ON THE IMPACT OF PERSONAL FREEDOM ON

VOTER PARTICIPATION OF ELIGIBLE VOTERS IN PRESIDENTIAL ELECTIONS

by

Kimberly Diane Bynum

A Dissertation Submitted in Partial Fulfillment

Of the Requirements for the Degree

Doctorate of Business Administration

Department of Economics

Davis College of Business

Jacksonville University, Jacksonville, FL

2017

APPROVED BY:

_____Dr. Richard Cebula, Committee Chair

_____Dr. Robert Boylan, Committee Member

_____Dr. Robert Houmes, Committee Member

ABSTRACT

This dissertation extends the rational voter model to include a measure of personal freedom which captures certain motivations not previously accounted for in prior empirical studies of voter turnout in U.S. presidential elections. Fixed-effects estimations of a panel data set of publicly available data reflecting explanatory variables for the 50 states for the presidential election years 2000, 2004, 2008, 2012, and 2016 suggest that this previously unaccounted-for variable, personal freedom (PERSONAL_F), may exercise a negative and statistically significant influence on the expected benefits of voting and hence a negative and statistically significant impact on the voter participation rate. State-level empirical evidence is presented to support the hypothesis that, after allowing for a variety of other factors, greater personal freedom decreases voter participation, *ceteris paribus.*

Keywords: expected benefits of voting, personal freedom, voter participation

Dedication

I dedicate my dissertation work to my family and many friends and supporters. A special feeling of gratitude to my husband, J. T. Bynum, who bore the brunt of my frustration and anxiety, taking care of the kids, home and me singlehandedly throughout this three-year journey. For my Aunt Karen and Uncle John, who sowed seeds of time, money and resources to set me up for academic success, not just with this specific achievement of a doctoral degree, but for my success in life, in general. For Dr. Valerie Rao, my favorite Medical Examiner and former boss, who insisted that I enroll in the Jacksonville University DBA graduate program, and supported me with time off work and endless words and acts of encouragement.

I dedicate this work and give special thanks to my amazing daughter, Tess, for motivating me with her determination and work ethic in gymnastics, and especially for being okay with not having Mom around to do the normal things a mom should do while I completed my doctoral program. You have been my loudest cheerleader, biggest supporter, and my greatest source of inspiration.

Acknowledgments

I would like to thank each of the members of my advisory committee: Dr. Richard Cebula, Dr. Robert Boylan, and Dr. Robert Houmes. Your input and assistance in completing this project has been invaluable. I would like to especially thank Dr. Richard Cebula for his guidance throughout this dissertation process. He has been a tremendous source of knowledge and wisdom both as a professor and as an advisor. I am grateful for the time that he devoted to me through editing, discussion, and instruction over the past several months. I could not have completed this program without his assistance.

I would also like to thank the other outstanding professors I have had the opportunity to work with at Jacksonville University through coursework: Dr. Barry Thornton, Dr. Donnie Horner, and Dr. Doug Johannsen, each of whose insights and instruction have benefitted me, both academically and personally. In addition, I would like to recognize the profound impact of Andre J. van Rensburg and the entire DBA Cohort 1 on my academic and professional development. I will be eternally grateful for the inspiration, encouragement, and loyalty this group has unconditionally provided to me throughout this journey. It is my sincere hope that this work lives up to the high standards and expectations that these extraordinary professors and my peers have set.

Table of Contents

List of Tables

List of Figures

CHAPTER ONE: INTRODUCTION

The Problem of Explaining Voter Turnout

Effectively explaining voter behavior is a topic that continues to challenge and confound researchers from academic disciplines ranging from marketing (consumer behavior) to political scientists to economists. Although barriers to voting in the United States, including polls taxes, suspension of literacy tests, lowering the age of voter eligibility and lowering state residency requirements have been significantly eliminated or reduced over the past 100 years, Americans continue to show up at voting booths in smaller numbers than in most other democratic nations (Ashenfelter & Kelley, 1975; Tolbert & Smith, 2005). As low voter turnout rates become the norm with each passing U.S. presidential election, there has been increased interest in developing theories that help explain and better understand voter behavior. Even after decades of experimentation resulting in conflicting findings (Cebula, 2004; Copeland & Laband, 2002; Everson, 1981; Magleby, 1984; Smith, M., 2001; Tolbert, 2003), researchers continue to search for the most efficient model that will adequately explain voter behavior. Of course, this line of inquiry raises the question: "Why is voter turnout a matter of interest?"

Political Scientists' Perspective on Voter Turnout

For political scientists, the impetus for understanding voter behavior is often related to better understanding and finding ways to increase voter turnout; however, these researchers argue among themselves whether increased voter turnout adds value to the political process and/or benefits the American political system. For those political scientists who perceive lower turnout rates as a positive, reasons cited range from minimizing democratic participation of uneducated voters (Jakee & Sun, 2006; Leighley, 1991), to political stability because of citizens being content with the political system (Krauthammer, 1990). On the other side of the debate,

Dalton (2008) and Teixeira (1992) argue in favor of studying voter behavior with the intent of increasing voter turnout to prevent an erosion of the culture of democracy that has defined the United States as Americans become disenfranchised with government and withdraw or disengage from politics altogether.

Economist's Perspective of Voter Turnout

From an economist's perspective, the importance of voter behavior in presidential elections and turnout in those elections tend to be relevant for much more practical reasons. Simply stated, voter turnout affects presidential election outcomes, and presidential election outcomes have profound implications on the economy, foreign policy, regulatory matters. and resource allocation, all of which all in turn affect business. Huber and Kirchler (2013) note, "Politics and business are intertwined in many ways… politicians and business owners exert considerable influence on one another" (p. 285). Alesina's (1987) Rational Partisan Theory suggests that "election outcomes may trigger temporary changes in real macroeconomic variables" (Heckelman, 2001, p. 417). The following text provides empirical studies and real-world examples that support these concepts.

Economic Impact of Voter Turnout

"Participatory democracy theory," said to be coined by Arnold Kaufman in 1960, occurs where "democracy is control by citizens of their own affairs, which sometimes, though not always, involves instructing governmental bodies to carry out citizens' wishes" (Cunningham, 2002, p. 26). Matsusaka (1995) describes direct democracy as a "public decision-making process in which enactment of laws depends on a direct vote of citizens, not their elected representatives" (p. 591). He demonstrates empirically that participatory democracy, as a means of impacting fiscal behavior through citizen-led initiatives and voting behavior, can result in the following forms of economic outcomes at the state level: 1) lower spending per capita; 2) a shift away from state spending to local spending; and 3) less reliance on taxes for revenue and more on charges for services (p. 617).

There is a major body of economics and business literature that address various forms of economic freedom, each of which is often affected by political outcomes resulting from election outcomes, and which in turn affect business formation, location, and success or failure. The literature "shows that countries with institutions consistent with the principles of economic freedom tend to experience higher growth rates, less unemployment, and higher investment in human, physical, and social capital" (Nicolaev & Bennett, 2015, p. 40). Additional studies by Stansel, Torra, and McMahon (2016 and earlier); Gwartney, Lawson, and Hall (2016 and earlier), and Cebula, Hall, Mixon, and Payne (2015) provide a broad and in-depth set of insights into this election outcome/economic decision-making business context.

A very specific example of voting behavior driven by economic motivation can be seen in the 1860 and 1864 presidential elections, in which northern counties with large manufacturing interests in the South shifted their votes from Democrat to Republican by 2.25% (Liscow, 2012). This shift stemmed from the manufacturing interests' desire to keep the South in the Union, which was the Republican position at the time. Three economic reasons are cited by Liscow (2012) to explain this shift of voter patterns in the North: 1) To protect Northern manufacturers from possible import tariffs being placed on their goods being sold in the South, which would have put them on a level playing field with the Europeans, removing the economic advantage that tariff-protected goods provided; 2) To protect against a "long, porous southern border, which may have promoted smuggling of goods northward, causing prices to drop; and 3) To ensure northern manufactures retained access to the South's primary goods, especially cotton (pp. 39-40). This historical example of voter behavior emphatically demonstrates the causal relationship, whether perceived or actual, between election results and economic outcomes.

Political business cycles (PBC's), defined by Verstyuk (2004) as "the regular influence of political factors – elections and government change - on the behavior of measures of economic activity (e.g., output, unemployment, inflation, stock indexes) and policy instruments (including government spending, taxation, interest rates, monetary base, exchange rates)" are phenomena exemplifying the impact that politics has on economics (pp. 169-170). Verstyuk (2004) observes that "the relationship between economic expectations and voting decisions is especially robust for presidential elections" (p. 170). The author empirically shows that "expected inflation rate, expected unemployment rate, as well as contemporaneous inflation rates and unemployed rates are significant factors of voters' decision, purporting that people tend to vote for the left party (Democrats) when unemployment is expected to be high, and for the right party (Republican) when inflation is expected to be high" (p. 179). Empirical testing in both industrialized and developing countries, as presented by Block and Vaaler (2001), also supports traditional PBC theory which predicts that monetary and fiscal policies will be expansionary just prior to elections and contractionary afterwards. Another area impacted by political business cycles is that of regulatory review, which is considered in the next paragraph.

Regulatory Impact of Voter Turnout

The result of a presidential election will have significant impact on regulatory matters. In fact, Shamoun and Yandle (2016) declare that "exercising White House control by way of regulatory review is central to a President's political success" (p. 89). Whether nominating positions that will affect regulations (think Secretary of Agriculture, Secretary of Commerce, Secretary of Labor, Secretary of Energy, Security of Homeland Security, Secretary of Education etc.) as a newly elected President or participating in the regulatory review process, expected presidential actions motivate voter intentions. The 2016 presidential election provides several examples of regulatory voting expectations as motivators of voter participation. The candidates' views regarding immigration laws, health care policies, Supreme Court Justice nominations, income tax laws, and environmental regulations, and voters' expectations of how a newly elected president would manage these regulatory issues certainly impacted voter turnout and behavior. (Pew Research Center, 2016).

Resource Allocation Impact of Voter Turnout

In addition to impact on regulatory matters, Cebula (2008) notes that "…election outcomes can have very profound implications for societal and government resource allocations" (p. 302). Presidential candidates tend to land somewhere along a continuum between purely free markets and somewhat non-market (socialist) economies. In a free-market economy, the determination of what is to be produced and of the corresponding allocation of resources (land, raw materials, machinery, and other "capital,") is largely unhampered by government rationing, price-fixing, or other external controls. Allocation is determined solely through intrinsic market processes. By contrast, primarily non-market economies resource allocation is accomplished primarily through government command. Federal budget allocations to the state is a practical application of election outcomes influencing resource allocations. A Larcinese, Rizzo, and Testa (2006) study shows that U.S. Presidents (in addition to numerous other institutional players) are engaged in the tactical distribution of federal funds to the states. The authors empirically show that states that display large support for the presidential party tend to be rewarded, while states which are predominantly opposed to the President tend to be penalized (p. 454).

Research Question: Does Personal Freedom Impact Voter Turnout?

This introduction serves to demonstrate the profound impact of presidential elections on the economy, regulatory matters, and resource allocation, which all, in turn, affect business. Thus, the study of voter turnout is relevant beyond the political scientist's realm. As an economist seeking to study how society distributes resources, such as land, labor, raw materials, and machinery, to produce goods and services, one cannot ignore the impact of politics. The aim of this dissertation is to extend the rational voter model to include a measure of personal freedom, which captures motivations not previously accounted for in empirical studies of voter turnout in presidential elections. Empirical evidence is presented to support the hypothesis that greater personal freedom decreases voter participation, *ceteris paribus*. Potential business impacts of decreased voter participation will also be discussed.

This dissertation consists of five chapters. In this introductory chapter, an overview of the research problem and research question has been explained. Chapter Two provides a literature review of relevant voter behavior theories and models. Subsequently, in Chapter Three, the central hypothesis is developed; furthermore, the modeling analysis in Chapter Three identifies the control variables in the model to be estimated, along with a description of the variables and data for the estimations. Chapter Four introduces the findings using fixed-effects estimations of publicly-available data reflecting explanatory variables for the 50 states for presidential election years 2000, 2004, 2008, 2012, and 2016. Finally, Chapter Five summarizes

the results of the study and provides policy implications thereof.

CHAPTER TWO: LITERATURE REVIEW

Aldrich (1993) reminds the reader that "voting is … less well understood and explained empirically than other political acts engaged in regularly by citizens" (p. 246). From a rational perspective, if voting is costly for the individual (time, money, resources, intangibles), and the probability of one individual vote impacting the outcome of an election is near zero, then logically an individual should not vote. And while voter turnout has declined through the years since 1960, people do continue to participate in U.S. presidential elections. This chapter examines both mainstream theoretical models and empirical studies that attempt to explain this "voter paradox".

Rational Voter Model (RVM)

The Rational Voter Model (RVM), introduced by Downs (1957), and used in this study as the model in which hypotheses are grounded, is represented as a mathematical equation in which the probability that an eligible voter will vote is a positive function of the gross benefits associated with voting and a negative function of the expected costs associated with voting. Expected costs of voting include costs of obtaining information and determining how to vote, costs of registering to vote, and costs of going to the polls. Even citizens who choose to abstain pay some form of decision-making cost associated with deciding whether they do want to vote (Aldrich, 2003, p. 248). One would expect that as costs of voting increase, voter turnout decreases.

The Rational Voter Model may be represented by the equation:

$R = pB - C$, where

R = the probability that the voter will turn out

p = the probability that an individual's act of voting will determine the outcome of the election

B = an individual's benefit derived from the election outcome occurring to his or her liking

C = costs of voting (time/effort spent)

From a mathematical perspective, the probability of one's vote "mattering" in an election (determining the outcome) is approximately zero. Therefore, the pB (expected benefit) is approximately zero. If pB = 0, then R = - C, so by the Rational Voter Model, one would expect that the logical person would not vote; however, that is certainly not the case. Aldrich (1993) addresses this apparent failure of Downs' (1957) Rational Voter Model through reinterpretation of the benefits of voting. The author first explains that political behavior (voting, specifically in this study), is predicated on preferences (attitudes, beliefs, values) which, in turn, determine behavior. This statement, which Aldrich (1993) claims "virtually all scholars agree with," parallels Fishbein and Ajzen's (1980) "Theory of Reasoned Action" (TRA)." TRA states that a specific behavior, in this case voting in a presidential election, is best approximated by a person's intention to engage in that behavior. A person's intention is determined by his or her attitudes and beliefs toward the behavior in question. According to de Run and Ting (2014), beliefs are "mostly defined as specific statements about the attributes of objects, and they are antecedents of attitude (p. 467). If one can uncover the beliefs held toward a specific behavior, then presumably one can more effectively influence and affect that behavior. See Figure 2.1.

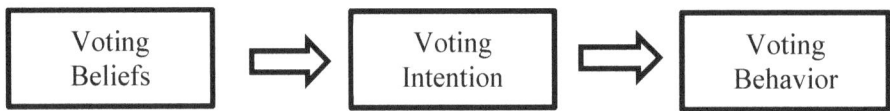

Figure 2.1 This figure illustrates the application of the Theory of Reasoned Action to voting behavior.

Aldrich (1993) argues that "rational choice theory is just about how these preferences determine behavior" and suggests that Downs' original theory simply needs to be completed (p. 247) by broadening earlier interpretations of benefits of voting. From a utility standpoint, he argues that voter turnout is "a low-cost, low-benefit action... Small changes in costs and benefits alter the turnout decision for many citizens" (p. 261). Aldrich (1993) goes on to conclude that most of the explanation for voting may be found in the "intrinsic values of voting" (i.e., in the C and D terms)

An early extension of Downs' (1957) model, as expanded by Riker and Ordeshook (1968), is

$R = \{pB + D\} > C$, where for voting to occur

the (p)robability the vote will matter "times" the (B)enefit of one candidate winning over another, combined with the feeling of fulfilling one's civic (D)uty, must be greater than the (C)ost of voting. In the past 50 years since Downs (1957) and Riker and Ordeshook (1968) first described the RVM, numerous researchers have offered extensions and empirical studies to better understand, explain and predict why people vote (Aldrich, 1993; Ashenfelter & Kelly, 1975; Brazel & Silberberg, 1973; Buchanan & Tullock, 1962; Copeland & Laband, 2002; Cox & Munger, 1989; Green & Shapiro, 1994; Greene & Nikolaev, 1999; Lapp, 1999; Ledyard, 1984; Morton, 1987; Piven & Cloward, 1988; Teixeira, 1992; Wolfinger & Rosenstone, 1980;). The majority of these researchers utilized a broad interpretation of voting costs and benefits and included socioeconomic and demographic variables such as unemployment rate, median household income, education attainment level, female labor force participation rates, race, gender, marital status, age, and others to explain and/or predict voter turnout. Results were sometimes inconsistent, and most models had little explanatory power (low $R^{2)}$.

Matsusaka and Palda (1999) suggest two paths for future research to better explain voter behavior: (1). Continue to search for new explanatory variables and away from reliance on traditional demographics like age and income, or (2). Move toward the study of aggregated voting behavior, where individual idiosyncrasies will cancel each other and allow the estimation of models with greater explanatory power (p. 442). Researchers have begun to consider new explanatory variables that expand the cost-benefit calculation to include intangible benefits of voting such as completing a duty or obligation and the desire to express one's self, among others. Research considering these determinants has led to the development of the Expressive Voting Theory, discussed next.

Expressive Voter Model (EVM)

Fischer (1996) divides motives for voting into two categories: instrumental and expressive. Instrumental votes can impact the outcome of the election (cost versus benefit), whereas expressive votes allow individuals to achieve some additional benefit, not necessarily related to the outcome of the election. Hamlin and Jennings (2011) expand on this concept defining behavior as purely expressive in nature only when the action is [perceived to be] inconsequential (p. 8). In the instance of voting, if one believes that his or her one vote will not change or sway the election, yet chooses to vote regardless of this belief, then the act of voting is defined to be "expressive" in nature. Rather than an expected outcome from a person's act of voting, the person votes because of the significance of the act of voting by itself, and is not tied to a particular outcome.

In EVM, voting behavior is grounded in the premise that "rational, self-interested individuals sometimes, perhaps often, engage in behavior that is not motivated directly by a benefit cost calculation. Behavior may be expressive, in the sense that the actions taken simply cannot influence an outcome" (Copeland & Laband, 2002, p. 351). The Expressive Voter Model (EVM) expands the Rational Voter Model to test "non-traditional and non-demographic variables" to ascertain additional determinants of voter participation rates (Cebula, 2004, p. 215). Copeland and Laband's (2002) Expressive Voter Model is written as:

Turnout = f (expressiveness, closeness of race, other established factors)

where 'other established factors' include age, educational attainment and other demographic variables previously explored in the Rational Voter Model. The expressive determinants, to be more fully developed later in this paper, may include political expressiveness, sense of duty or obligation, closeness of election, and newly introduced in this paper, personal freedom (Cebula, 2001; Cebula, Duquette, & Mixon, 2013; Cebula & Hulse, 2007; Copeland & Laband, 2002; Levine & Palfrey, 2007; Matsusaka & Palda, 1993). To build on the theoretical underpinnings of voter behavior, several empirical studies relating to variables included in the Expressive Voter Model, as well as the Rational Voter Model, are discussed next.

EVM Empirical Studies

The 1982 Nuclear Freeze Referendum (NFR) provides a relevant example of an initiative purely expressive in nature. In this referendum, the largest single-issue initiative in the U.S.' history at that time, there were no budgetary, expenditure or policy consequences attached to the measure. In other words, no real resources were to be expended as a result of the passage of this initiative. Based on this criterion, Feigenbaum, Karoly, and Levy (1988) present the 1982 NFR as "an ideal case for isolating expressive conduct at the polls…where the only outcome would be words, not deeds" (pp. 201-202). The authors explain, "The expressive model contends that when voting is costless, people do not have interests, but rather, moral judgements which now

23

cost very little to express" (p. 212). Their empirical studies seemed to conclude that when a voter's choice appears to neither cost nor benefit the individual, "moral expression dominates consequentialist behavior" (p. 212), thereby supporting the EVM.

To test the EVM using political expressiveness as a dependent variable, Copeland and Laband (2002), choose two proxies to represent political expressiveness: (1) whether the respondent displayed a button/sticker/sign prior to the election, and (2) whether the respondent donated money to the Federal Election Commission on his/her federal income tax return (Copeland & Laband, 2002, p. 356). Both proxies were shown to have a positive and significant correlation to the propensity to vote. Most notably, respondents who reported displaying buttons, stickers and/or signs were 40% more likely to vote…than individuals who did not report displaying campaign button/stickers/signs" (Copeland & Laband, 2002, p. 359).

In his extension of Copeland and Laband's (2002) studies, Cebula (2004) hypothesizes that "voter participation rates will be elevated by an increased degree of expressive behavior (of the emotions associated with presidential campaigning, polling, nomination, and actual voting) during presidential election years (p. 216). Leveraging aggregate time series analysis from 1960-1996, Cebula (2004) measures voter participation rates against issues evoking emotional responses such as the Vietnam War, the Watergate scandal, the public's dissatisfaction with government, and the opportunity to participate in presidential elections. Even after controlling for economic variables such as inflation, personal income tax progressivity, and unemployment rate, Cebula's (2004) findings suggest that non-socioeconomic issues "can invoke such emotionalism as to profoundly affect the public's decision whether to vote or not, despite the negligible probability that any individuals vote could affect the outcome of an election… and proved to significantly influence the aggregate voter participation rate" (pp. 215, 219).

Prior literature also indicates that the expected closeness of an election results in greater voter participation (Cebula, 2001; Cebula et al., 2013; Cebula & Hulse, 2007; Levine & Palfrey, 2007; Matsusaka & Palda, 1993). Closeness of an election is measured by "the expected vote share differential between the two political parties" (Ashworth, Geys, & Heyndels , 2006, p. 386). Ashworth et al., (2006) explores the role of electoral closeness in the context of expressive voting, in which the motivation to vote is not directly tied to a cost-benefit calculation. The authors explain that expressive voters find utility in identifying with a particular group, regardless of whether they believe their vote will ultimately affect the outcome.

In presidential elections, individual states in which the general elections are "close", based on either polling prior to the election and/or actual voting results post-election, are dubbed 'battleground states.' Cebula, et al., (2013) presents "the battleground voting hypothesis," which argues that "the greater the degree to which a given state is a battleground state, the greater the expected benefits from voting in that state and hence the greater the turnout in that state" (p. 3795). The empirical results suggest that the "battleground state effect" generates an average of 7.8 additional percentage points in voter participation in presidential elections over the period 1964–2008 for those states at the top of the scale. Finally, Carporale and Poitras (2014) analyze a time series model of voter turnout for 34 U.S. presidential elections, 1880–2012 and find the expected closeness of the outcome significantly influences voter turnout (p. 3637).

RVM Empirical Studies

Whereas the Expressive Voter Model uses variables such as political expressiveness and closeness of the election to explain voter turnout, the earlier Rational Voter Model utilizes socio-economic determinants such as income level, education attainment level, ethnicity, age, the female labor force participation rate and unemployment rate. Previous studies of the impact of these determinants on voter turnout (Barreto, Segura, & Woods, 2004; Caporale & Poitras, 2014; Cebula, 2004; Cebula, Angjellari-Dajci, & Rossi, 2016; Cebula & Toma, 2006; Fedderson, 2004; Tolbert & Smith, 2005; Wolfinger & Rosenstone, 1980), provide the following consistent empirical results: as the minority ethnic population increases, voter turnout decreases, *ceteris paribus*; as age increases, voter turnout increases, *ceteris paribus*; as the female labor force participation rate increases, voter turnout increases, *ceteris paribus;* as unemployment rate increases, voter turnout increases, *ceteris paribus*; and, as household income increases, voter turnout decreases, *ceteris paribus.* This dissertation will rely upon, and accept findings from the previous research on these socio-economic-demographic variables.

This literature review explains the foundation for this dissertation's voter participation model. Socio-economic-demographic variables are included from the Rational Voter Model portion of the literature review, expressive variables from the Expressive Voter Model are also included, and finally, a new expressive variable, personal freedom, is added to this dissertation's extended voter turnout model. A description of each of the variables included in this dissertation's voter turnout model, and suggested reasoning behind the empirical findings of the new and extended model, will be further developed in Chapter Three.

CHAPTER THREE: METHODOLOGY

Initial Framework for Personal Freedom

In this chapter, the initial framework for the central hypothesis is developed and the research question is explicitly defined. A thorough description of all variables is provided, along with support from previous empirical findings for each of the control variables' impact on voter turnout. No prior empirical results are available for the 'PERSONAL_F' variable, which is newly added in this study's voter model and will be discussed first. Finally, the data used for the estimations is presented in table format. Table 3.1 provides a list of variables and each variable's description and sources. The raw data used for the estimations is provided in Appendix A.

Table 3.1

List of Variables with Descriptions and Data Sources

Variable Name	Variable Description	Data Source
VEP	% population eligible to vote that actually turnout to vote	http://www.electproject.org/home/voter-turnout/voter-turnout-data
PERSONAL_F	Personal Freedom	CATO Institute Ruger & Sorens (2016) www.freedominthe50states.org
MED_HH_INC	Median HH Income	U.S. Census Bureau, Current Population Survey, Annual Social and Economic Supplements Table H-8 http://www.census.gov/data/tables/time-series/demo/income-poverty/historical-income-households.html
BACH_DEG	% pop w/ Bachelor degree or higher	U.S. Census Bureau, Current Population Survey Table 13
UR	Unemployment rate	Bureau of Labor Statistics, Current Population Survey
FLFPR	Female labor force participation rate	Bureau of Labor Statistics, Current Population Survey
AFAM	% population African American	U.S. Census Bureau, American Community Survey Table S0103
CLOSEELEC	Closeness of election	American Research Group Polling >5% difference between candidates' pre-election polling = Not Close = 0; <5% difference = Close = 1

This study extends both the Rational Voter and Expressive Voter models to include a measure of personal freedom ('PERSONAL_F'), which captures certain motivations not previously accounted for in prior empirical studies of voter turnout in U.S. presidential elections. In this extended model, the voting decision is still considered a traditional cost-benefit analysis, in which one will vote if and only if the perceived benefits of voting outweigh perceived costs. However, to fully incorporate both RVM and EVM models, the list of perceived costs and benefits is widened so that voter turnout is considered to be a function of expressiveness, socio-economic-demographic factors, as well as public choice control variables. Additionally, this study includes a heretofore understudied expressive variable, personal freedom ('PERSONAL_F'), to more fully explain voter turnout. This updated model is expressed as:

Voter Turnout = f(expressiveness, socio-economic-demographic factors,

public choice control variables)

Voter turnout is defined as a function of expressive, socio-economic-demographic factors, and public choice control determinants. The expressiveness component is captured in the personal freedom ('PERSONAL_F') variable. Socio-economic factors include income, education, unemployment rate, female labor force participation rate, and ethnicity. Finally, the public choice control variable is represented by the variable, closeness of election ('CLOSEELEC').

As noted in Chapter Two, prior empirical studies have shown consistent and statistically significant relationships between voter turnout and closeness of election, as well as between voter turnout and socio-economic variables. However, an extensive review of the body of literature concerned with voter turnout and determinants of voter turnout reveals a potential additional expressive variable that to date, has been either understudied or ignored: personal freedom. To determine whether personal freedom is a relevant explanatory variable that might

be included in models attempting to explain voter turnout, the following model will be estimated:

Voter Turnout = f (personal freedom, income, education, unemployment rate, female labor

force participation rate, ethnicity, closeness of election)   (2)

VEP = f (PERSONAL_F, MED_HH_INC, BACH_DEG, UR, FLFPR, AFAM, CLOSEELEC)   (3)

The Research Question

Controlling for socio-economic-demographic and public choice control variables

determined in previous research to have a statistically significant impact on voter turnout, does

the independent variable, PERSONAL_F, exhibit a negative and statistically significant impact

on voter turnout, as hypothesized?

H1: PERSONAL_F will have a negative and statistically significant effect on VEP, *ceteris paribus*

Ancillary Research Questions

Do each of the following independent variables exhibit expected positive(negative) and

statistically significant impact on voter turnout, consistent with previous empirical studies?

H2a: MED_HH_INC will have a negative and statistically significant effect on VEP, *ceteris paribus*

H2b: BACH_DEG will have a positive and statistically significant effect on VEP, *ceteris paribus*

H2c: UR will have a positive and statistically significant effect on VEP, *ceteris paribus*

H2d: FLFPR will have a positive and statistically significant effect on VEP, *ceteris paribus*

H2e: AFAM will have a positive and statistically significant effect on VEP, *ceteris paribus*

H2f: CLOSEELEC will have a positive and statistically significant effect on VEP, *ceteris paribus*

The remainder of this chapter will label and define each dependent and independent

variable, explain how each variable has been shown to impact voter turnout in previous studies,

and provide the methodology, source of and actual data used in this study's estimations.

Description of Variables

Personal Freedom ('PERSONAL_F')

This dissertation's central hypothesis for the variable Personal Freedom ('PERSONAL_F') reads: the greater the personal freedom measured in an individual state, the lower the expected benefit of voting, and thus, the lower the expected voter turnout in that state. To effectively address this question, the definition of personal freedom, as well as the source of measuring the personal freedom variable, should first be well defined and understood. The following section provides this information.

The Cato Institute, founded in 1977, is a public policy research organization—a think tank— whose scholars and analysts conduct independent research on a wide range of policy issues. Most notably, the Cato Institute publishes a bi-annual Index named, "Freedom in the 50 States: An Index of Personal and Economic Freedom" which ranks the American states according to how their public policies affect individual freedoms in the economic, social, and personal spheres. The authors note, "…social scientists will benefit from the index, because it is an open question how individual liberty relates to phenomena such as economic growth, migration, and partisan politics in the American states. In the same way, although political scientists may value democracy for its own sake, they can also research empirically what causes democracy and how democracy affects other phenomena" (Ruger & Sorens, 2016, p. 7).

Authors of the Personal and Economic Freedom Index, Rugers and Sorens (2016), define "freedom" as a moral concept - the ability to pursue one's ends without unjust interference from others. They ground their definition of freedom within an individual rights framework. In their opinion, "individuals should not be prevented from ordering their lives, liberties, and property as they see fit, so long as they do not infringe on the rights of others" (p. 5). Ruger and Sorens compute an inclusive freedom index, named 'overall freedom index', as well as three additional separate indices which each capture a specific dimension of 'overall freedom.' The 'overall freedom index' is calculated by combining values computed in the following three separate, individual indices: 1). fiscal policy, 2). regulatory policy, and 3). personal freedom. To calculate these individual indices of freedom, the authors weight public policies per the estimated costs of government restrictions on the specific freedom imposed. These costs are then aggregated from the three individual indices to calculate the 'overall freedom index.' Each of the three individual indices: fiscal policy, regulatory policy and personal freedom compose approximately one third each of the 'overall freedom index.' To be clear, this dissertation utilizes the Cato Institute's personal freedom index, which is just one of three dimensions of freedom used to compute the overall freedom index.

The personal freedom dimension consists of the following categories: gun policy, alcohol policy, marijuana-related policy, travel policy, gaming policy, mala prohibit a and miscellaneous civil liberties, education policy, civil asset forfeiture, law enforcement statistics, marriage policy, campaign finance policy, and tobacco policy. Weighting these categories is noted to be subjective because the observable financial impacts of these policies often do not include the full harms to citizens (p. 3). Despite this subjectivity in weighting, the Ruger and Sorens (2016) indices (economic and personal freedom) arguably provide dependable, accurate and robust representations of personal freedom, and is the only index to measure at the state level; therefore, this index is utilized in this study of determinants of voter turnout (Cebula, 2014) Weighting for each area of personal freedom are represented graphically in Figure 3.1.

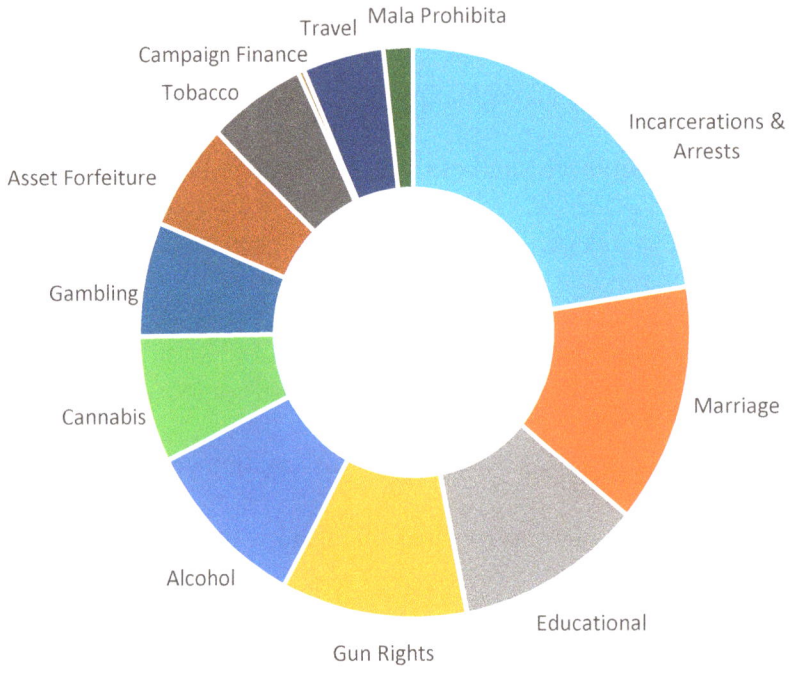

Personal Freedom Weightings
Ruger & Sorens (2016)

Travel · Mala Prohibita · Campaign Finance · Tobacco · Asset Forfeiture · Gambling · Cannabis · Alcohol · Gun Rights · Educational · Marriage · Incarcerations & Arrests

Figure 3.1. Weighting of personal freedom components

For a complete breakdown of percentages and detailed information regarding the factors used to compute each of the personal freedom components represented in Figure 3.1, see Appendix B.

Extending Downs' (1957) Rational Voter Model to include "expressiveness" (which is captured in the 'PERSONAL_F' variable in this study) as an additional benefit of voting offers a reasonable explanation as to why "rational, self-interested individuals sometimes, perhaps often, engage in behavior that is not motivated directly by a benefit-cost calculation" (Copeland & Laband, 2002, p. 351), as it relates to presidential election voting. The authors argue that expressive voting provides inherent value to the voter, not because the act of voting is expected to influence the outcome of the election, but because the act of voting allows one to express his/her themselves with respect to the candidate or issues at hand. Additionally, the authors go on to state, "It seems plausible to suggest that declining voter turnout may reflect a generally increasing happiness among prospective voters with their lot in life, with a consequent decline in their motivation to be politically expressive" (p. 360). This caveat provided by Copeland & Laband (2002) explains in part why, in this study, greater personal freedom is expected to have a negative effect on voter turnout. If a citizen feels that he has all the personal freedom he desires, there is no perceived benefit to voting in a presidential election as a means to express himself. Using the personal freedom index developed by Ruger and Sorens (2016) within an otherwise conventional voter turnout model allows an empirical investigation as to whether voter turnout in U.S. presidential elections is significantly negatively (positively) impacted by higher (lower) levels of personal freedom.

It should be noted that extensive search of prior literature regarding the impact of personal freedom on voter turnout failed to uncover empirical studies directly related to this topic. Databases searched include ABI/Inform Complete, Business Source Complete, and ProQuest Central, the largest multidisciplinary database with full text articles from over 8,000 journals and newspapers, covering over 160 subject areas. Although empirical findings to allow for a direct comparison were not discovered, a few articles that may provide anecdotal evidence for this dissertation's personal freedom voter turnout hypothesis will be discussed next. For example, Cebula and Mixon (2012) study the impact of ending the military draft on aggregate voter participation rate. Using data from U.S. national elections between 1948 and 2006, in which 1948 through 1972 experienced military conscription (versus an all-volunteer army), they investigate the hypothesis that the elimination of the military draft in the U.S. acted to reduce expected benefits from voting, and thereby reduced the aggregate voter participation rate. Using a dummy variable to represent the election years that military conscription was either active or inactive, this study shows this variable accounts for a 9.68 percentage-point reduction in voter turnout due to the elimination of military conscription (Cebula & Mixon, 2012, p. 336). One might argue that the existence of a mandatory draft (military conscription) reduces one's personal freedom, while the elimination of the same increases one's personal freedom. If this argument is accepted as valid, Cebula and Mixon's (2012) findings support this study's hypothesis that greater personal freedom results in lower voter turnout. In another article discussing the historic low voter turnout in the 1996 presidential election, Carlin (1996) theorizes that the "hypertrophy of personal freedom…where personal liberty has been absolutized…has become a sacred cow, an idol to which unqualified deference must be paid" as one of the major reasons why Americans are "disengaging from the body politic," (p. 6). While not an empirical study, these statements from Carlin (1996) may also provide an anecdotal basis for supporting the hypothesis that greater personal freedom results in lower voter turnout. Voter turnout, the dependent variable in this study, is discussed next.

Voter Turnout ('VEP')

The dependent variable, 'VEP', measures voter turnout in U.S. presidential elections. As Tolbert and Smith (2005) note in their study on voter turnout, "traditionally, turnout has been calculated simply as a ratio between the number of people who voted and the number of Americans of voting age" (p. 292). However, McDonald and Popkin (2001) argue that this measure includes people who are ineligible to vote – most notably noncitizens and felons, and thus create an estimate of turnout by removing ineligible voting populations from the population estimates, voter eligible population ('VEP'). This seemingly more accurate representation of turnout is chosen as the measure to be utilized for voter turnout in U.S. presidential elections in this study and may be retrieved from The United States Election Project at

http://www.electproject.org/home/voter-turnout/voter-turnout-data.

Median Household Income ('MED_HH_INC')

The expected cost of voting may be represented in various forms; however, this study

focuses on the median household income by state ('MED_HH_INC'). A median household

income refers to the income level earned by a given household where half of the homes in the

area earn more and half earn less. Median household income is used instead of the average or

mean household income because it can give a more accurate picture of an area's actual economic

status.

The Current Population Survey (CPS) is the source of the official Government statistics

on employment and unemployment and has been conducted monthly for over 50 years.

Although the main purpose of the survey is to collect information on the employment situation, a

secondary purpose is to collect information on the demographic status of the population,

information such as age, sex, race, marital status, educational attainment, income and family

structure. The CPS sample is based on the civilian non-institutional population of the United

States and is in 826 sample areas comprising 1,328 counties and independent cities with

coverage in every State and in the District of Columbia. For this study, Table H-8, Median

Household Income by State, is the source of the 'MED_HH_INC' variable. This table reports, in

dollars, the current median household income adjusted for the previous year's measured rate of

inflation in the Consumer Price Index.

From 1960 to present, previous empirical studies suggest that voter participation rates are

positively related to income among the electorate (Campbell et al., 1960; Tolbert et al., 2003;

Tolbert & Smith, 2005). However, recent empirical studies on the impact of income on voter turnout have proposed that a higher income may result in a higher opportunity cost of voting, or perhaps higher income people may perceive themselves as too busy to vote (Cebula et al., 2016). Voter participation rates have been shown to be negatively related to income (Cebula, 2004; Cebula & Toma, 2006). Based on these conflicting prior empirical findings, one could hypothesize either way. However, based on the most recent findings, this study hypothesizes that the higher the 'MED_HH_INC' in a state, the lower the 'VEP' in that state, *ceteris paribus*.

Percentage of Population with a Bachelor's Degree or Higher ('BACH_DEG')

In this study, educational attainment is measured using the variable 'BACH_DEG' which represents the percentage of the population of a particular state that has earned a bachelor's degree or higher. In previous voter turnout empirical studies, education attainment level has shown to be statistically significant and positively associated with voter turnout. From a cost-benefit perspective, Cebula et al., (2016) states, "it is argued that the higher the level of educational attainment, the greater may be the expected gross and thus net benefits from voting, *ceteris paribus*" because the greater may be one's knowledge of and appreciation of the significance of participating *per se* in the electoral process in a democratic society" (p. 4). The study also suggests that an expressive benefit of fulfilling one's civic duty may also be tied to higher levels of educational attainment. Other empirical studies that support the ancillary hypothesis that the independent variable, 'BACH_DEG' will have a positive and statistically significant effect on VEP, *ceteris paribus,* include: Cebula, 2004; Cebula & Toma, 2006; Copeland & Laband, 2002; and Tolbert et al., 2001.

Unemployment Rate ('UR')

The 'UR' variable is measured using the annual average unemployment rate, by state, of the civilian non-institutional population as reported in Table 14 from the Bureau of Labor

Statistics. Cebula et al., (2016) hypothesize that higher unemployment rates result in voters perceiving greater gross and net benefits from voting, whether by expressing dissatisfaction with the unemployment rate or expressing desire for a change at some level to improve employment opportunities. Similarly, Caporale and Poitras (2014) find that economic adversity (as measured by unemployment rates) drives increased voter turnout. Smith (2001) and Cebula et al., (2013) also provide empirical evidence in agreement with the positive impact of the unemployment rate on voter turnout. Based on these previous findings, voter participation rate is expected to be positively impacted by 'UR' in this study.

Female Labor Force Participation Rate ('FLFPR')

The female labor force participation rate represents the number of people who are actively participating in or desire to be participating in the work force. These people are either actively seeking employment or are employed, and are at or about the working age of 16 years of age. People not included in the participation rate include those who do not want to work or cannot work. This includes people such as students, homemakers, incarcerated people and retirees. To be clear, those who have no job and are not looking for one—are counted as *not* in the labor force. In this study, 'FLFPR' may be retrieved from the Bureau of Labor Statistics.

Putnam (2000) observes "...people active in the workforce are more involved in community life... [and that] the movement of women toward professional equality has tended to increase their civic involvement," with voting being "...the most common form of political activity" (p. 35). Cebula and Toma (2006, p. 35) argue that as the 'FLFPR' rises, the percent of the female population in the workforce rises and "...arguably thereby becomes more/better informed on and arguably more sensitive to a host of labor market and economics issues..." Women in the workplace may perceive an increased benefit of voting to protect their best interests and therefore increase their participation in the electoral process. In other words, increased labor force participation by women may elevate their expected benefits from voting, *ceteris paribus*. This study concurs with previous empirical finding which hypothesizes that 'FLFPR' will have a positive and statistically significant effect on 'VEP', *ceteris paribus*.

Percent Population of African Americans ('AFAM')

It has been argued by Barreto et al., (2004) that if potential voters feel disenfranchised from their government because of the government's perceived unresponsiveness to their needs, they may react emotionally with respect to voting by becoming more apathetic. This expectation of lower voting in response to disenfranchisement is also supported by the findings in Cebula and Toma (2006). According to Barreto et al., (2004), disenfranchisement is often the perspective of the African American population in the United States. Cebula et al., (2016) describe their two-part disenfranchisement/enfranchisement hypothesis, explaining that minorities who feel politically disenfranchised have lower expected benefits from voting and have a lower participation rate, while on the other hand, minorities who feel potentially enfranchised or empowered by a candidate sharing their own minority status, have higher expected benefits and hence are more inclined to go to the polls. Hence, the higher the percentage of a state's population accounted for by African Americans, the lower the voter participation rate is expected to be, *ceteris paribus*. In this study, the percentage of the African American population by state is recorded from the U.S. Census Bureau, American Community Survey Table S0103.

However, this study includes presidential election years 2008, 2012, and 2016, in which an ethnic minority, Barack Obama, was either on the ballot or still in office. One can argue that based on this unique circumstance, the African American population, previously disenfranchised with the government may have felt enfranchised or empowered due to one of the presidential candidates sharing its specific minority status. This enfranchisement or empowerment may increase the perceived expected benefit of voting for the African American population, resulting in an increase in African American voter participation rate, *ceteris paribus.* In this study, the explanatory variable 'AFAM' is expected to have a negative impact on VPR for the election years prior to 2008, and a positive impact on VRP for the election years 2008, 2012, and 2016, offsetting the overall negative impact to VPR found in previous empirical studies.

Closeness of Election ('CLOSEELEC')

Closeness is used as a measure of the competitiveness of an election and is commonly used in empirical models of turnout (Caporale, 2014). The closer an election is perceived to be, the greater the probability that a single vote may influence the outcome of an election. The higher probability of influencing the outcome of the election increases the perceived benefit of voting to the individual. A meta-analysis by Ashworth, Geys, and Heyndel (2006) finds that 52 out of 83 studies that use aggregate vote data include some measure of closeness, and this makes closeness "by far the most analyzed element in the turnout literature" (p. 647). However, quantifying closeness of an election is a subjective exercise. For example, Cebula et al., (2013) express the degree to which an individual state may be considered a battleground state as $S = N / M$, where S is the state's Score, N represents the number of that state's Electoral College votes, and M is the popular vote margin of victory. States are then ranked in descending order to determine which are 'battleground states' and by definition, this list identifies which states are expected to have "close" general election results. In comparison, Matsusaka and Palda (1993) described three different measures of "closeness" included in their study, but stated, "…the ideal measure would be survey predictions from opinion polls taken the day before the election" (p.

862). Incidentally, Cebula and Hulse (2007) use state-level, pre-election polls as a proxy for election closeness to hypothesize that the greater (or lower) the ratio of the two leading presidential candidates in any given state, the lower (or higher) the aggregate voter participation would be in that state, *ceteris paribus* (p. 36).

In this study, a dummy variable measuring election closeness (named 'CLOSEELEC') is calculated utilizing available pre-election polling data closest to the actual election date. If polling data reveals a five percent or less differential between the two leading presidential candidates, 'CLOSEELEC' is assigned a 1. If the polling data reveals a greater than five percent differential between the two leading presidential candidates, a 0 is assigned. The construct validity, defined as whether a scale or test measures the construct adequately, of the 'CLOSEELEC' variable is assessed by examining how it related to the 'battleground' states identified throughout the 2000-2016 presidential elections. The expected outcome is that where a state is assigned 'CLOSEELEC' equal to 1, that the state would also be considered a 'battleground state.' This expectation was confirmed by the data, suggesting the dummy variable, 'CLOSEELEC' exhibits construct validity. In this study, 'CLOSEELEC' is hypothesized to be statistically significant and positively correlated to voter turnout.

With the research question defined, and variables in the model described, the following paragraphs introduce the study's methodology to outline the steps and scientific methods used by the researcher. First, the general philosophy regarding the methodology of economics and econometrics is discussed, followed by an introduction of the empirical model chosen to examine the relationship between personal freedom and voter participation in this study. Finally, the results of the model estimation, as calculated using Eviews™ statistical software, is provided.

The Methodology of Econometrics

Mark Balaug (1992) defines the methodology of economics as:

> A study of the relationship between theoretical concepts
>
> and warranted conclusions about the real world; in particular,
>
> methodology is that branch of economics where we examine
>
> the ways in which economists justify their theories and the
>
> reasons they offer for preferring one theory over another;
>
> methodology is both a descriptive discipline – "this is what most
>
> economists do" – and a prescriptive one – "this is what
>
> economists should do to advance economics." (p. xii)

There are at least three objectives (other than testing theories) for econometrics. First, econometrics may be used to measure unknown values of theoretically defined parameters or unobservable variables. Second, econometrics may be used to predict the value of a variable. This prediction may be based directly on a prior economic theory or it may be an atheoretical statistical exercise. The economist James Heckman (2000) provides an important clarification, however, for what distinguishes econometrics from statistics: econometrics focuses on establishing causation, while statistics is content with correlation (p. 45). Finally, econometrics may be used to characterize a relationship or phenomenon. Econometrics packages the data in a way that reveals relationships that, in turn, become the foundation for theory (Hoover, 2005, p. 8).

Blaug (1992) also notes that econometrics relies on observational data rather than data collected from controlled experiments. This is not unusual, in that numerous other scientific disciplines, including sociology and political science also rely on observational data (Wold,

1969). Due to the reliance on observational data rather than the use of controlled experiments, regression analysis is a commonly used statistical method of econometricians. Regression analysis is a statistical process for estimating the relationships among variables. This tool is utilized when the focus is on the relationship between a dependent variable and one or more independent variables. Regression analysis explains how the value of the dependent variable changes when any one of the independent variables is varied, while the other independent variables are held fixed (Ramcharan, 2006). This dissertation research will follow the econometrics logical positivism tradition, specifically by utilizing fixed-effects estimation on publicly available data to test the hypothesis that greater personal freedom does, in fact, decrease voter participation rates during presidential election years in the United States, while controlling for other independent variables.

While Tolbert et al., (2003) suggest aggregate-level analyses may be subject to ecological fallacies, in which inferences about the nature of individuals (individual voters, in this case) are deduced from inference for the group to which those individuals belong (VEP, in this case), other researchers suggest that the ecological correlation gives a better picture of the outcome of public policy actions, thus they recommend the ecological correlation over the individual level correlation for this purpose (Lubinski & Humphreys, 1996). Because this dissertation's aim is to estimate the impact of personal freedom on voter turnout as a means for considering how this turnout ultimately influences public policy, aggregate-level analysis appears to be an appropriate method for this study, based on Lubinski and Humphreys, 1996. This study's balanced panel data, or longitudinal data, consists of a time series (2000, 2004, 2008, 20012, 2016) for each statistical unit (dependent and all independent variables) in the cross section (states).

The Theoretical Model

$$\text{VEP}jk = a_0 + a_1\text{PERSONAL\_F}jk + a_2\text{MED\_HH\_INC}jk + a_3\text{BACH\_DEG}jk + a_4\text{UR}jk +$$

$$a_5\text{FLFPR}jk + a_6\text{AFAM}jk + a_7\text{CLOSEELC}jk + \varepsilon \qquad (4)$$

The precise definitions of the variables in Eq. 4 are, as follows:

VEPjk	percentage of eligible voters that voted in state j in year k
a_0	constant term
PERSONAL_Fjk	measure of personal freedom in state j in year k
MED_HH_INCjk	median household income in state j in year k
BACH_DEGjk	percentage of population with bachelor's degree or higher in state j in year k
URjk	average annual unemployment rate in state j in year k
FLFPRjk	female labor force participation rate in state j in year k
AFAMjk	percentage of African American population in state j in year k
CLOSEELECjk	measure of the closeness of the election in state j in year k
εj	stochastic error term

Data Analysis Methods

EViews statistical software computes panel equation estimation using linear or nonlinear squares or instrumental variables (two-stage least squares), with correction for fixed or random effects in both the cross-section and period dimensions. In this dissertation, the data are analyzed using panel least squares regression analysis with correction for fixed effects. To choose between fixed and random effects model, one must examine the correlation between the errors and the regressors in the model using the Hausman Test (Hausman, 1978). The null hypothesis of the Hausman Test is that there is no correlation between the errors and the regressors, and therefore the preferred model is random effects. The alternate hypothesis is that the preferred model is fixed effects. As evidenced by the results of the Hausman Test found in Table 3.2 in which the p-value of the null hypothesis is less than 0.05 at 0.0045, the null hypothesis must be rejected. Thus, the fixed effects model is the appropriate choice.

Table 3.2

Hausman Test Results

Correlated Random Effects - Hausman Test			
Test Summary		Chi-Sq. Stat	Prob.
Cross-section random		20.546947	0.0045 p < .05

Cross-section random effects test comparisons:

Variable	Fixed	Random	Var(Diff.)	Prob.
BACH_DEG	0.007267	0.006401	0.000002	0.498
CLOSEELEC	0.016985	0.021731	0.000007	0.0647
FLFPR	0.002492	0.004382	0.000001	0.0862
PERSONAL_F	0.273641	-0.157234	0.001284	0.0012
UR	0.006727	0.008099	0	0.0058
MED_HH_INC	0	0	0	0.3822
AFAM	0.002855	-0.000576	0.000032	0.5436

As another argument for choosing the fixed effects correction, when the model is known to have omitted variables, and these variables are correlated with the variables in the model, as is the case in this study, the fixed effects correction is chosen as a means for controlling for omitted variable bias. Additionally, as a means of correcting for heteroskedasticity, the Pearson method for computing coefficient covariance is selected.

To test for the causal relationship between personal freedom and voter participation rates (VEP), secondary data was collected for the 50 states over the period of 2000-2016 during U.S. presidential election years (every four years). Presidential election years were chosen for two reasons. First, as noted in Tolbert and Smith (2005), "previous research on voter turnout suggests that presidential and midterm elections must be analyzed separately, given the substantially higher turnout in presidential elections across states" (p. 296). Cebula (2004) attributes this phenomenon to "an increased degree of expressive behavior (of the emotions associated with presidential campaigning, polling, nomination and actual voting) during presidential election years" (p. 216). To mitigate the impact that increased contributions, campaigning and other methods of driving citizens to the voting booths may have on VPR during presidential election year as compared to off years, midterm national elections data is not included in this study.

Although the more traditional VPR calculation is a ratio of the number of people who voted to the number of Americans of voting age (VAP), McDonald and Popkin (2001) noted that VAP includes ineligible voters such as noncitizens and felons. To more accurately reflect the percentage of voter turnout, the dependent variable chosen for this study was VEP (Voter Eligible Population), which removes the ineligible noncitizens and felons from the population estimate. Testing for causal relationship between personal freedom and VEP also requires the researcher to control for other independent variables. To this end, data collection includes personal freedom measured by state, as well as socio-economic, demographic and public choice variables suggested in earlier studies to influence voter turnout. No data outliers are observable based on visual review of the raw panel data. See Table 3.1 for a list of all variables, variable descriptions, and variable data sources. The raw panel data is listed in Appendix A.

In summary, this chapter explains the methodology used in this study to explore the effect of personal freedom on voter participation rates in presidential elections, while controlling for other independent variables known to impact VEP. The next chapter, Chapter Four,

discusses the findings obtained using this methodology.

CHAPTER FOUR: FINDINGS

The focus of this dissertation was the impact of personal freedom on voter turnout, while controlling for numerous socio-economic-demographic and public choice variables. Based on the framework below, voter turnout ('VEP') is potentially influenced not only by personal freedom ('PERSONAL_F'), but also by the values of 'MED_HH_INC,' 'BACH_DEG,' 'UR,' 'FLFPR,' 'AFAM,' and 'CLOSEELEC.' The estimations provided in this study involve the following empirical model:

$$VEP_{jk} = a_0 + a_1PERSONAL\_F_{jk} + a_2 MED\_HH\_INC_{jk} + a_3BACH\_DEG_{jk} + a_4 UR_{jk} +$$

$$a_5FLFPR_{jk} + a_6AFAM_{jk} + a_7CLOSEELEC_{jk} + \varepsilon \qquad (5)$$

where a_0 = constant term and ε = the stochastic error term.

Based on earlier discussion, the expected signs on the coefficients in equation (5) are as follows:

$$a_1 < 0, \ a_2 < 0, \ a_3 > 0, \ a_4 > 0, \ a_5 > 0, \ a_6 > 0, \ a_7 > 0 \qquad (6)$$

Results

The initial results of the formal empirical analysis of equation (5) is provided in Table 4.1, where estimated coefficients, t-values and probability values are listed. Seven of seven estimated coefficients on the explanatory variables exhibit the expected signs, with three of these coefficients being statistically significant at the 1% level ('PERSONAL_F', 'BACH_DEG, 'UR''), one being statistically significant at the 5% level ('CLOSEELEC'), and one being statistically significant at the 10% level ('FLFPR'). Of note, 'MED_HH_INC' and 'AFAM' fail to be statistically significant. With an R^2 equal to 83.3 and F-stat of 17.2, the model appears to adequately explain the variation in the dependent variable, 'VEP.'

Table 4.1

Panel Estimation Results, Presidential Election Years, 2000-2016
Annual Data Dependent Variable: VEP

Variable	Coefficient	t-Statistic	Prob.	
C	0.19601	1.51449	0.1315	
AFAM	0.00286	0.50178	0.6164	
BACH_DEG	0.00730	4.13295	0.0001	***
CLOSEELEC	0.01699	2.49999	0.0133	**
FLFPR	0.00249	1.63946	0.1027	*
MED_HH_INC	-1.72E-07	-0.35374	0.7239	
PERSONAL_F	-0.27364	-3.97757	0.0001	***
UR	0.00673	4.01485	0.0001	***

***statistically significant (s.s) at the 1% level;
** s.s. at the 5% level; * s.s at the 10% level

R-squared	0.83278
Adj R-squared	0.78427
F-statistic	17.16415
Prob(F-stat)	0.00000

Hypothesis(es)

Consistent with the main hypothesis, **H1: PERSONAL_F will have a negative and statistically significant effect on VEP,** *ceteris paribus,* the results of this study empirically illustrate that voter participation rates are significantly lower in states with higher personal freedom, controlling for variation due to socio-economic-demographic and public choice variables previously shown to impact turn out. This is the first known study to consider the effect of personal freedom on voter participation rates.

Table 4.2 records the percentage change in VPR for a 1% change in each explanatory variable by taking the log of the dependent variable, 'VEP'. With an R2 equal to 83.3 and F-stat of 17.2, the model also appears to adequately explain the variation in the dependent variable, 'Log(VEP).' Specifically, the model estimation shows a 1% change in the personal freedom variable ('PERSONAL_F') results in a 0.468% decrease in VEP, supporting the main hypothesis of this dissertation.

Table 4.2

Panel Estimation Results, Presidential Election Years, 2000-2016
Annual Data Dependent Variable: LOG(VEP)

Log(VEP)			
Variable	Coefficient	t-Statistic	Prob.
C	-1.19264	-5.33775	0.0000
AFAM	0.005457	0.555465	0.5792
BACH_DEG	0.012751	4.200418	0.0000
CLOSEELEC	0.026238	2.237024	0.0264
FLFPR	0.003848	1.466481	0.1441
MED_HH_INC	-3.80E-07	-0.45279	0.6512
PERSONAL_F	**-0.46813**	**-3.94152**	**0.0001**
UR	1.14E-02	3.948515	0.0001
	R-squared	0.826271	
	Adj R-sqrd	0.775863	
	F-statistic	16.39155	

Additionally, this study's empirical findings regarding the following ancillary research questions confirm earlier studies from which hypotheses were formed.

H2b: BACH_DEG will have a positive and statistically significant effect on VEP, *ceteris paribus.* At the 1% statistical significance level, the percentage of a state's population with a bachelor's degree or higher is positively related to voter turnout; that is, the higher the education attainment level in a state, other things held the same, the greater the voter turnout; and **H2c: UR will have a positive and statistically significant effect on VEP,** *ceteris paribus.*

At the 1% statistical significance level, a state's unemployment rate is positively related to voter turnout; that is, the higher the unemployment rate in a state, other things held the same, the greater the voter turnout; and **H2d: FLFPR will have a positive and statistically significant effect on VEP,** *ceteris paribus.* At the 10% statistical significance level, a state's female labor force participation rate is positively related to voter turnout; that is, the higher the female labor force participation rate in a state, other things held the same, the greater the voter turnout; and **H2f: CLOSEELEC will have a positive and statistically significant effect on VEP,** *ceteris paribus.* At the 5% statistical significance level, a state's closeness of election is positively related to voter turnout; that is, the closer an election in a state, other things held the same, the greater the voter turnout.

Finally, two ancillary research questions, addressing explanatory variables consistently shown to have specific and consistent impacts on voter participation rates failed to be statistically significant. These hypotheses are listed next:

H2a: MED_HH_INC will have a negative and statistically significant effect on VEP, *ceteris paribus.* Median household income was not statistically significant, although it did exhibit the expected sign.

H2e: AFAM will have a negative and statistically significant effect on VEP, *ceteris paribus.* The percentage of African American population failed to be statistically significant, although it did exhibit the expected sign.

Descriptive Statistics

For the interested reader, Table 4.3 lists descriptive statistics for the model. Skewness and kurtosis have been included to provide comparison of the variables' statistical distribution shape to the normal distribution. Skewness has a value of 0 and kurtosis has a value of 3 in the normal distribution.

Table 4.3

Descriptive Statistics, 2000 - 2016, Presidential Election Year Data

	VEP	AFAM	BACH_DEG	CLOSEELEC	FLFPR	MED_HH_INC	PERSONAL_F	UR
Mean	0.6033	10.1932	27.2544	0.2920	60.0236	48933	0.0074	5.3616
Median	0.6030	7.1000	26.6000	0.0000	59.9500	47779	0.0008	5.2000
Std. Dev.	0.0675	9.4962	4.9684	0.4556	4.4205	9362	0.0676	1.6488
Skewness	-0.1105	1.1157	0.3160	0.9149	0.0059	0.4333	0.2248	0.6938
Kurtosis	2.8773	3.3782	2.7903	1.8371	2.6026	2.8897	2.7657	3.4458

Next, Table 4.4 provides the correlation matrix for the explanatory variables. The correlation matrix shows the strength and direction of a linear relationship between two variables, also referred to as collinearity. Values range from 1, which represents a perfectly positive linear relationship, to -1, which represents a perfectly negative linear relationship between two variables. A 0 represents no linear relationship. Typically, correlation matrix values greater than 0.5 and less than -0.5 are considered to be threshold values indicating potential collinearity issues in the model. Collinearity increases the standard errors of the coefficients and by overinflating the standard errors, it may make some variables statistically insignificant when they should be significant. For most of the explanatory variables in Table 4.4, there is little evidence of collinearity; however, there is evidence of some collinearity between 'MED_HH_INC' and 'BACH_DEG,' as demonstrated by the Table 4.4 value of 0.7525.

Table 4.4

Correlation Matrix, Explanatory Variables 2000-2016, Presidential Election Years, Annual Data

	AFAM	BACH_DEG	CLOSEELEC	FLFPR	HISP	MED_HH_INC	PERSONAL_F	UR
AFAM	1.0000							
BACH_DEG	-0.1496	1.0000						
CLOSEELEC	0.0018	-0.0031	1.0000					
FLFPR	-0.4082	0.3484	0.0161	1.0000				
HISP	-0.1326	0.1863	0.0854	-0.2443	1.0000			
MED_HH_INC	-0.1901	**0.7525**	0.0653	0.2958	0.1441	1.0000		
PERSONAL_F	-0.3488	0.3289	0.1390	0.1166	0.1978	0.2713	1.0000	
UR	0.2475	-0.0375	0.0321	-0.4445	0.2173	0.0410	0.0661	1.0000

To determine whether this collinearity between 'MED_HH_INC' and 'BACH_DEG' is an issue in the final model, the variance inflation factor (VIF) is calculated. If the VIF is equal to one, there is no multicollinearity among the variables; however, if the VIF is greater than one, the variables may be moderately correlated. A VIF between five and ten indicates high correlation that may be problematic. If the VIF is greater than ten, one may assume the regression coefficients are poorly estimated due to multicollinearity. Table 4.54 provides the VIF for each of the independent variables. The largest VIF values, neither of which indicate problematic correlation, are 'BACH_DEG' VIF equal to 2.6362, and 'MED_HH_INC' VIF equal to 2.1459. While moderate correlation exists between 'MED_HH_INC' and 'BACH_DEG,' multicollinearity between the two variables does not appear to be a significant issue in this dissertation's model.

Table 4.5

Measuring Multicollinearity using Variance Inflation Factor

Variance Inflation Factors	
Variable	VIF
C	NA
AFAM	1.4248
BACH_DEG	2.6362
CLOSEELEC	1.0340
FLFPR	1.7444
MED_HH_INC	2.1459
PERSONAL_F	1.1881
UR	1.2483

Robustness Checks

To examine structural validity of the model, several robustness checks are conducted. First, the 'PERSONAL_F' coefficient estimate is observed to examine how it behaves when the regression is modified by adding or removing regressors. The following regressors are removed individually, 'BACH_DEG', 'CLOSEELEC', 'MED_HH_INC', 'FLPR', and 'UR'. Next, the following explanatory variables not included in this study's model, but often used in other VPR empirical models are added to the model to test for robustness: percentage of a state's population age 65 years older ('65PLUS') and percentage of a state's population with a high school diploma or higher ('HS_GRAD'). Regardless of added or removed regressors in the model, the 'PERSONAL_F' remains statistically significant at the 1% level and R^2 remains consistent between 81 and 83% are recorded in Table 4.6, suggesting robustness, or strength, of the model.

Table 4.6

Robustness Checks Utilizing Various Regressors (for 'VEP')

			PERSONAL_F STATISTICS			
	Coeff	t-stat	Prob	R-squared	F-Stat	Prob(F-stat)
Full Model	**-0.2736**	**-3.9776**	**0.0001**	**0.8328**	**17.1642**	**0.0000**
AFAM Removed	-0.2729	-3.9751	0.0001	0.8326	17.5393	0.0000
BACH_DEG Removed	-2.18E-01	-3.1051	0.0022	0.8180	17.5531	0.0000
CLOSEELEC Removed	-0.2770	-3.9737	0.0001	0.8274	16.9051	0.0000
MED_HH_INC Removed	-0.2734	-3.9830	0.0001	0.8327	17.5531	0.0000
FLFPR Removed	-0.2906	-4.2545	0.0000	0.8305	17.2770	0.0000
UR Removed	-0.3148	-4.4573	0.0000	0.8188	15.9408	0.0000
65_PLUS Added	-0.2836	-4.0984	0.0001	0.8341	16.9293	0.0000
HS_GRAD Added	-0.2796	-4.0185	0.0001	0.8331	16.8157	0.0000

Table 4.6 reveals consistent values for the 'PERSONAL_F' variable coefficients, t-statistics and probabilities, thereby suggesting the structural validity of the estimated model.

To summarize the findings reported here in Chapter Four, the explanatory variable of emphasis in this study, 'PERSONAL_F', proves to be statistically significant and have a negative impact on voter turnout, as hypothesized. As mentioned previously, this empirical study is the first to include personal freedom as an explanatory variable in a model estimating voter turnout. Additionally, results of other explanatory variables included in the study's model are consistent with previous empirical studies, except for 'AFAM' and 'MED_HH_INC' which prove to be statistically insignificant in this particular model. The following chapter will conclude with a discussion of implications and limitations of this study, as well as ideas for future related research.

CHAPTER FIVE: CONCLUSIONS

Overview

This chapter will provide a summary in the Discussion section that includes findings and conclusions based upon the research presented. Practical suggestions to address several of the issues mentioned in the paper will be discussed in the Implications section, and limitations of the study will also be addressed. Finally, ideas for future research will be presented.

Discussion

As voter turnout rates in U.S. presidential elections continue to decline, there has been continued interest in developing and expanding theories that help adequately explain voter behavior. Researchers continue to search for the most effective model to represent voter behavior as evidenced by voter participation rates. This study extends both the Rational Voter and Expressive Voter models to include a measure of personal freedom ('PERSONAL_F'), which captures certain motivations not previously accounted for in prior empirical studies of voter turnout in U.S. presidential elections. The results of the formal empirical analysis are provided in Table 4.1, where voter participation rate ('VEP') is found to be statistically significant and negatively impacted by higher levels of personal freedom. Because this is the first known study to include personal freedom as a determinant in voter turnout, no previous results are available for comparison.

In this study's expanded model, the voting decision is still considered a traditional cost-benefit analysis, in which one will vote if and only if the perceived benefits of voting outweigh perceived costs. However, to fully incorporate both RVM and EVM models, the list of perceived costs and benefits is broadened so that voter turnout is considered to be a function of expressiveness, socio-economic-demographic factors, as well as public choice control variables.

As noted in Chapter Two, prior empirical studies have shown consistent and statistically significant relationships between voter turnout and closeness of election, as well as between voter turnout and socio-economic variables. This study confirms prior studies' findings for closeness of election ('CLOSEELEC'), level of education attainment ('BACH_DEG'), female labor force participation rate ('FLFPR') and unemployment rate ('UR'). Two variables typically found to be significant in other voter models fail to be significant in this study: ethnic minority population ('AFAM') and income level ('MED_HH_INC'). With an R^2 equal to 83.3 and F-stat of 17.2, the model appears to adequately explain the variation in the dependent variable, 'VEP.'

Implications

As noted in Chapter One, voter turnout affects presidential election outcomes, and presidential election outcomes have profound implications on the economy, foreign policy, regulatory matters, and resource allocation. The voter turnout model presented in this dissertation is based upon the premise that voter turnout is a crucial phenomenon to understand, predict, and potentially influence because of these far-reaching implications of election outcomes. Explaining voter turnout with a valid and reliable model is an important step in better understanding how to predict and influence voter turnout. This study presents a previously underexplored explanatory variable, personal freedom, to assist in explaining voter turnout. Based upon this study's empirical findings, personal freedom, as calculated by Ruger & Sorens (2016), and represented in this study's voter turnout model as the explanatory variable 'PERSONAL_F', may be a relevant determinant to include in future voter participation models. As a reminder, the personal freedom construct consists of the following categories: gun policy, alcohol policy, marijuana-related policy, travel policy, gaming policy, *mala prohibit a* and miscellaneous civil liberties, education policy, civil asset forfeiture, law enforcement statistics, marriage policy, campaign finance policy, and tobacco policy. If increased personal freedom in a state lowers voter participation rates, what does this mean for the future of the democratic process? While Dalton (2008) and Teixeira (1992) argue in favor of studying voter behavior with the intent of increasing voter turnout to prevent an erosion of the culture of democracy, some political scientists perceive lower turnout rates as a positive, equating lack of voter participation to political stability because of citizens being content with the political system (Krauthammer, 1990). From a practical standpoint in which voter participation is understood to impact policy decisions, understanding the relationship between personal freedom and voter turnout is a first step in attempting to leverage this relationship to impact voter behavior.

Limitations

The measurement of the personal freedom variable relies exclusively on the Ruger and Sorens (2016) definition and calculation of personal freedom at the state level, which may be considered a limitation, as there is no other available source from which to compare and validate Ruger and Sorens' personal freedom calculations. At the time of this research, other indices of freedom, such as The Fraser Institute's Economic Freedom Index, the State of the World Liberty Index, and Freedom House's Civil Liberty Index provide national measures of freedom, however, not at the U.S. state level, as was used in this dissertation (Graeff, 2004). With state-level data for personal freedom currently unavailable, an achievable mitigation tactic may be to vary the weightings of the various components that comprise Ruger and Sorens (2016) personal freedom measurement, and use these re-calculated personal freedom results to examine the impact on voter turnout for consistency. Additionally, the Ruger and Sorens (2016) personal freedom index is only available for the years 2000-2016. Although there is no impact to this research based on the 2000-2016 data availability, this limitation does prevent examination of the impact of personal freedom on voter turnout in presidential election years prior to 2000.

Another limitation in this study may be a lack of inclusion of certain explanatory variables such as the effect of increased campaign contributions and political communications (including social media use) on voter turnout in presidential elections. In previous literature, these two explanatory variables are purported to lower educative costs (a cost of voting), increase perceived benefits of voting due to a more informed voter, and hence, increase voter turnout (Baek, 2009; Barton, Castillo, & Petrie, 2014; Grober & Schram, 2006). Adding state-level data to include these two variables may increase the R^2 value of the extended model. However, one could argue that the aggregate effect of these two variables may already be partially captured in the 'CLOSEELEC' variable.

Recommendations for Future Research

Although this study's model includes mainstream socio-economic-demographic variables, as well as the newly introduced 'PERSONAL_F' explanatory variable, the model for voter turnout can most certainly be expanded or modified. As mentioned in the Limitations section, the impacts of campaign contributions, political communications, social media, and numerous other expressive variables may be added to the model to consider their impacts on voter turnout. Additionally, explanatory variables that have long had consistent impacts on voter turnout in previous studies may need to be re-examined as societal context changes. For example, African Americans may have been motivated to vote due to "enfranchisement" by having African American, Barack Obama, participate in recent presidential elections, significantly altering the expected turnout rates for this ethnic group. As other minority groups are represented (Hispanic, females, etc.), will this same phenomenon of increased voter participation apply? Additionally, now that African Americans have engaged in the political process in increasing number, will the repeat-voting-habit persistence phenomenon, as introduced by (Cebula, Durden, & Gaynor, 2008) come into play? Another explanatory variable with long-standing positive impact on voter turnout to be re-examined may be female labor force participation rates (FLFPR). As women gain social and economic equality, and labor force participation rates level out, how will this impact overall voter turnout?

One's understanding of voter behavior is unquestionably linked to researchers' ability to capture motives that motivate citizens to vote. As earlier voter models are expanded to include socio-economic-demographic variables, as well as a plethora of ever-evolving expressive measures, researchers should also carefully consider how the continuous morphing of America's societal context will also impact aggregate voter behavior. These shifts in the fabric of American society, perhaps already manifested as enfranchisement of minority groups and by perception of increased personal freedom, should continue to be observed and incorporated into future models of voter behavior.

REFERENCES

Aldrich, J. H. (1993). Rational choice and turnout. *American Journal of Political Science*, *37*(1), 246.

Alesina, A. (1987). Macroeconomic policy in a two-party system as a repeated game, *Quarterly Journal of Economics, 102*(3), 651-678.

Allison, P. D. (2009). *Fixed effects regression models: Quantitative applications in the social sciences*. Sage Publications. Thousand Oaks, CA.

Ashenfelter, O., & Kelley, S., Jr. (1975). Determinants of participation in congressional elections. *Journal of Law and Economics, 18*: 695-733.

Ashworth, J., Geys, B., & Heyndels, S. (2006). Everyone likes a winner: An empirical test of the effect of electoral closeness on turnout in a context of expressive voting. *Public Choice, 128,* 383–405. doi: 10.1007/s11127-005-9006-8

Baek, M. (2009). A comparative analysis of political communication systems and voter turnout. *American Journal of Political Science, 53*(2), 376-393. doi:10.1111/j.1540-5907.2009.00376.x

Bailey, D., & Katz, J. N. (2011). Implementing panel-corrected standard errors in R: The PCSE package. *Journal of Statistical Software, Code Snippets, 42*(1), 1–11.

Barreto, M. A., Segura, G. M., & Woods, N. D. (2004). The mobilizing effect of majority-minority districts on Latino turnout. *American Political Science Review, 98*, 65-76.

Barton, J., Castillo, M., & Petrie, R. (2014). What persuades voters? A field experiment on political campaigning. *Economic Journal, 124*(574), F293-F326. doi:10.1111/ecoj.12093

Beck, N., & Katz, J. (1995). What to do (and not to do) with time-series-cross-section data in comparative politics. *American Political Science Review, 89*, 634-647.

Blaug, M., & de Marchi, N. (Eds.) (1991). *Appraising economic theories: Studies in the application of the methodology of research programs.* Aldershot: Edward Elgar.

Block, S., & Vaaler, P. M. (2001). The price of democracy: Sovereign risk ratings, bond spreads and political business cycles in developing countries. The Fletcher School of Law and Diplomacy: Tufts University: Medford, MA.

Bowler, S., & Donovan, T. (2004). Measuring the effect of direct democracy on state policy: Not all initiatives are created equal. *State Politics & Policy Quarterly, 4*(3), 345-363.

Brazel, Y., & Silberberg, E. (1973). Is the act of voting rational? *Public Choice, 16*, 51-58.

Buchanan, J., & Tullock, G. (1962). *The calculus of consent.* Ann Arbor: University of Michigan Press.

Caporale, T., & Poitras, M. (2014). Voter turnout in U.S. presidential elections: Does Carville's law explain the time series? *Applied Economics, 46*(29), 3630-3638. doi:10.1080/00036846.2014.937037

Carlin Jr., D. R. (1996). Democracy in decline. *Commonweal, 123*(21), 6.

Cebula, R. J. (2001). The electoral college and voter participation: Evidence on two hypotheses. *Atlantic Economic Journal, 29*(3), 304-310.

Cebula, R. J. (2004). Expressiveness and voting: Alternative evidence. *Atlantic Economic Journal, 32*(3), 215-220.

Cebula, R. (2014). The impact of economic freedom and personal freedom on net in-migration in the U.S.: A state-level empirical analysis, 2000 to 2010. *Journal of Labor Research, 35*(1), 88-103. doi:10.1007/s12122-014-9175-7

Cebula, R. J., Angjellari-Dajci, F., & Rossi, F. (2016). The disenfranchisement/enfranchisement voter participation rate hypothesis: Preliminary analysis. *International Journal of Applied*

*Economics, (13)*1, 1-14.

Cebula, R. J., Duquette, C. M., & Mixon, F. G. (2013). Battleground states and voter

    participation in U.S. presidential elections: An empirical test. *Applied Economics, 45*(26),

    3795-3799. doi:10.1080/00036846.2012.727981

Cebula, R. J., Durden, G. C., & Gaynor, P. E. (2008). The impact of the repeat-voting-habit

    persistence phenomenon on the probability of voting in presidential elections. *Southern*

    Economic Journal, 75(2), 429–440. Retrieved from

    http://www.jstor.org.ju.idm.oclc.org/stable/27751393

Cebula, R. J., Foley, M., & Hall, J. C. (2016). Freedom and gross in-migration: An empirical

    study of the post-great recession experience. *Journal of Economics and Finance, 40*(2),

    402-420. doi:http://dx.doi.org.ju.idm.oclc.org/10.1007/s12197-014-9315-1.

Cebula, R. J., Hall, J., Mixon, F. G., & Payne, J. E. (Eds.). (2015). *Economic behavior,*

    economic freedom, and entrepreneurship. Cheltenham, UK: Edward Elgar Publishing. doi:

    http://dx.doi.org/10.4337/9781784718237

Cebula, R. J., & Hulse, D. (2007). The poll results hypothesis. *Atlantic Economic Journal,*

    35(1), 33. doi:http://dx.doi.org.ju.idm.oclc.org/10.1007/s11293-006-9048-4.

Cebula, R., & Mixon, F. (2012). Dodging the vote? *Empirical Economics, 42*(1), 325-343.

    doi:10.1007/s00181-010-0415-2

Cebula, R. J., & Toma, M. (2006). Determinants of geographic differentials in the voter

    participation rate. *Atlantic Economic Journal, 34*(1), 33-40. doi:10.1007/s11293-006-6118-6

Copeland, C., & Laband, D. N. (2002). Expressiveness and voting. *Public Choice, 110*(3/4),

    351–363. Retrieved from http://www.jstor.org.ju.idm.oclc.org/stable/30026418

Cox, G. W., & Munger, M. C. (1989). Closeness, expenditures, and turnout in the 1982 U.S.

house elections. *American Political Science Review, 83*, 217-231.

Cunningham, F. (2002). *Theories of democracy: A critical introduction.* Routledge: NY.

Dalton, R. J. (2008). *The good citizen: How a younger generation is reshaping American politics*. CQ Press: Washington D.C.

deRun, E. C., & Ting, H. (2013). Generational cohorts and their attitudes toward advertising. *Trziste/Market Journal, 25*(2), 143-160.

Downs, A. (1957). *An economic theory of democracy*. New York: Harper and Row.

Everson, D. (1981). The effects of initiatives on voter turnout: A comparative state analysis. *Western Political Quarterly, 34*, 415-425.

Fedderson, T. J. (2004). Rational choice theory and the paradox of not voting. *Journal of Economic Perspectives, 18*, 99-112.

Feigenbaum, S., Karoly, L., & Levy, D. (1988). When votes are words not deeds: Some evidence from the nuclear freeze referendum. *Public Choice, 58*(3), 201-216. Retrieved from http://www.jstor.org.ju.idm.oclc.org/stable/30024929

Fischer, A. (1996). A further experimental study of expressive voting. *Public Choice, 88*(1/2), 171-184.

Fishbein, M., & Azjen, I. (1980). *Understanding attitudes and predicting social behavior.* Englewood Cliffs, NJ: Prentice-Hall.

Graeff, P. (2004). *Towards a worldwide index of personal freedom.* Fraser Institute. Retrieved from https://www.fraserinstitute.org/sites/default/files/ch4-measuring-individual-freedom.pdf

Green, D. P., & Shapiro, I. (1994). *Pathologies of rational choice theory: A critique of applications in political science*, New Haven: Yale University Press.

Greene, K. V., & Nikolaev, O. (1999). Voter participation and the redistributive state. *Public*

Choice, 98, 213-226.

Gwartney, J. D., & Lawson, R. A. (2003). The concept and measurement of economic

Freedom. *European Journal of Political Economy, 19*(3), 405–30.

Hall, J. C., & Lawson, R. A. (2014). Economic freedom of the world: An accounting of the

literature. *Contemporary Economic Policy, 32*(1), 1–19.

Hamlin, A., & Jennings, C. (2011). Expressive political behavior: Foundations, scope, and

implications. *British Journal of Political Science*. doi: 10.1017/S0007123411000020.

Hausman, J. A. (1978). Specification tests in econometrics. *Econometrica, 46*, 1251–1271.

Heckelman, J. D. (2001). The econometrics of rational partisan theory. *Applied Economics*,

(33), 417-426.

Heckman, J. J. (2000). Causal parameters and policy analysis in economics: A twentieth

century retrospective. *Quarterly Journal of Economics 115*(1), 45-97.

Hoover, K. D. (2005) *The methodology of econometric.* Prepared for the *Palgrave handbook of*

econometrics, Volume 1: Theoretical econometrics.

Huber, J., & Kirchler, M. (2013). Corporate campaign contributions and abnormal stock

returns after presidential elections. *Public Choice, 156*(1-2), 285-307.

doi:http://dx.doi.org.ju.idm.oclc.org/10.1007/s11127-011-9898-4

Jakee, K., & Sun, G., (2006). Is compulsory voting more democratic? *Public Choice, 53*, 61-

75.

Kahane, L. H. (2009). It's the economy, and then some: Modeling the presidential vote with state

panel data. *Public Choice, 139*(3-4), 343-356.

Krauthammer, C., (1990). In praise of low voter turnout. *Time, 21*, 82.

Larcinese, V., Rizzo, L., & Testa, C. (2005). *Allocating the U.S. federal budget to the states: The impact of the president*. St. Louis: Federal Reserve Bank of St Louis. Retrieved from

http://ezproxy.ju.edu:2048/login?url=http://search.proquest.com.ju.idm.oclc.org/docview/

1698329605?accountid=28468

Lapp, M., (1999). Incorporating groups into rational choice explanations of turnout: An

empirical test. *Public Choice, 98,* 171-185.

Leighley, J., (1991). Participation as a stimulus of political conceptualization. *Journal of*

Politics, 198-211.

Ledyard, J. (1984). The pure theory of two-candidate elections. *Public Choice, 44,* 7-41.

Levine, D. K., & Palfrey, T. R. (2007). The paradox of voter participation? A laboratory study.

The American Political Science Review, 101(1), 143-158. Retrieved from

http://ezproxy.ju.edu:2048/login?url=http://search.proquest.com.ju.idm.oclc.org/docview/214

434516?accountid=28468

Liscow, Z. (2012). Why fight secession? Evidence of economic motivations from the American

civil war. *Public Choice, 153*(1-2), 37-54.

doi:http://dx.doi.org.ju.idm.oclc.org/10.1007/s11127-011-9772-4

Lubinski & Humphries (1996). Seeing the forest from the trees: When predicting the behavior or

status of groups, correlate means. *Psychology, Public Policy, and Law, 2*(2), 363–376.

Magleby, D., (1984). *Direct legislation: Voting on ballot propositions in the United States.*

Baltimore: John Hopkins University Press.

Matsusaka, J. (1995). Fiscal effects of the voter initiative: Evidence from the last 30 years.

Journal of Political Economy, 103(3), 587-623. Retrieved from

http://www.jstor.org.ju.idm.oclc.org/stable/2138700

Matsusaka, J. G., & Palda, F. (1999). Voter turnout: How much can we explain? *Public*

Choice, 98(3/4), 431-446.

Matsusaka, J. G., & Palda, F. (1993). The downsian voter meets the ecological fallacy. *Public Choice (1986-1998), 77*(4), 855.

McDonald, M., & Popkin, S. (2001). The myth of the vanishing voter. *American Political Science Review, 95*, 963-974.

Morton, R. B. (1987). A group majority voting model of public good provision. *Social Choice and Welfare, 4,* 117-131.

Nikolaev, B., & Bennett, D. L. (2016). Give me liberty and give me control: Economic freedom, control, perceptions and the paradox of choice. *European Journal of Political Economy, (45)*, 39-52, Retrieved February 8, 2017 from http://www.sciencedirect.com/science/article/pii/S0176268016300611

O'Brien, R. M. (2007). A caution regarding rules of thumb for variance inflation factors. *Quality and Quantity, (41),* 673-690. doi:10.1007/s11135-006-9018-6.

Pew Research Center, (2016). Top voting issues of 2016. Retrieved from http://www.people-press.org/2016/07/07/4-top-voting-issues-in-2016-election/

Piven, F. F., & Cloward, R. (1988). *Why Americans don't vote*. New York: Pantheon. Putnam.

Ramcharan, R. (2006). Regressions: Why are economists obsessed with them? Retrieved October 31, 2016 from http://www.imf.org/external/pubs/ft/fandd/2006/03/basics.htm

Riker, W., & Ordeshook, P. (1968). A theory of the calculus of voting. *American Political Science Review 62*(1): 25-42.

Shamoun, D. Y., & Yandle, B. (2016). Asserting presidential preferences in a regulatory review bureaucracy. *Public Choice, 166*(1-2), 87-111. doi:http://dx.doi.org.ju.idm.oclc.org/10.1007/s11127-016-0316-9

Smith, M. A. (2001). The contingent effects on ballot initiatives and candidate races on turnout. *American Journal of Political Science, 43*(3), 700-706.

Stansel, D., & McMahon, F. (2013). Economic freedom of North America, 2013. Fraser Institute at: www.freetheworld.com/2013/efna/ EFNA2013-FINAL.pdf.

Stansel, D., Torra, J., & McMahon, F. (2014). Economic freedom of North America, 2014. Vancouver: Fraser Institute.

Stansel, D. B. (2013). An economic freedom index for U.S. metropolitan areas. *Journal of Regional Analysis & Policy, 43*(1), 3-20. Retrieved from http://ezproxy.ju.edu:2048/login?url = http://search.proquest.com.ju.idm.oclc.org/docview/1429687595?accountid=28468

Stansel, D. (2011). Why some cities are growing and others are shrinking. *Cato Journal, 31*(2), 285-303. Retrieved from http://ezproxy.ju.edu:2048/login?url=http://search.proquest.com.ju.idm.oclc.org/docview/875294404?accountid=28468

Teixeira, R. A. (1992). *The disappearing American voter*. Washington, D.C.: Brookings Institution.

Tolbert, C. J., & Smith, D.A. (2005). The educative effects of ballot initiatives on voter turnout. *American Politics Research, 33*(2), 283-309.

Verstyuk, S. (2004). Partisan differences in economic outcomes and corresponding voting behavior: Evidence from the U.S. *Public Choice, 120*(1-2), 169-189. Retrieved from http://ezproxy.ju.edu:2048/login?url=http://search.proquest.com.ju.idm.oclc.org/docview/

207196/864?accountid=28468

Wold, H. O. (1969). Econometrics as pioneering in non-experimental model building.

   Econometrica, 37(3), 369-381.

Wolfinger, R .E., & Rosenstone, S. J. (1980). *Who votes?* New Haven: Yale University Press.

Wooldridge, J. M. (2002). *Econometric analysis of cross section and panel data.* Cambridge,

   MA: The MIT Press.

APPENDICES

Appendix A

Panel Data, 2000-2016, U.S. Presidential Election Years, by State

State	Year	VEP	Personal F	UR	Med HH Inc	BACH_DEG	AFAM	FLFPR
AL	2000	51.6%	-0.0730814	4.6	$ 35,424	20.4	26.0	56.9
AL	2004	57.2%	-0.10124133	5.8	$ 36,629	22.3	26.1	55.8
AL	2008	60.8%	-0.12940127	5.6	$ 44,476	22.0	26.2	54.3
AL	2012	58.6%	-0.10769342	8.0	$ 43,464	22.3	26.5	52.0
AL	2016	58.9%	-0.08685432	6.1	$ 44,509	24.2	26.8	51.0
AK	2000	68.1%	0.112354722	6.6	$ 52,847	28.1	3.5	67.8
AK	2004	69.1%	0.080592874	7.5	$ 55,063	25.5	3.6	65.6
AK	2008	68.0%	0.048831027	6.8	$ 63,989	27.3	3.6	65.9
AK	2012	58.7%	0.056200182	7.4	$ 63,648	27.5	3.5	63.6
AK	2016	61.3%	0.132357183	6.7	$ 75,112	29.7	3.5	62.3
AZ	2000	45.6%	0.007357231	3.9	$ 39,783	24.6	3.1	56.6
AZ	2004	54.1%	-0.00600011	5.1	$ 43,846	28.0	3.4	57.4
AZ	2008	56.7%	-0.01935745	5.9	$ 46,914	25.1	3.6	57.1
AZ	2012	52.6%	0.032337513	8.2	$ 47,044	26.6	4.4	54.0
AZ	2016	54.3%	0.087584718	6.0	$ 52,248	27.7	4.4	53.9
AR	2000	47.9%	-0.03785992	4.4	$ 29,697	18.4	15.7	56.1
AR	2004	53.6%	-0.04131254	5.9	$ 34,984	18.8	15.6	54.9
AR	2008	52.5%	-0.04476517	5.2	$ 39,586	18.8	15.5	57.4
AR	2012	50.7%	-0.04111975	7.6	$ 39,018	19.8	15.7	54.1

69

AR	2016	52.6%	-0.02994278	5.2	$42,798	21.8	15.8	53.0
CA	2000	55.7%	0.030307448	4.9	$46,816	27.5	6.7	59.1
CA	2004	58.8%	0.021666929	6.2	$49,222	31.7	6.5	57.6
CA	2008	60.9%	0.013026411	7.1	$57,014	29.6	6.2	57.7
CA	2012	55.1%	0.060393287	10.4	$57,020	30.5	6.0	55.7
CA	2016	56.1%	0.085246722	6.2	$63,636	32.3	5.8	55.0
CO	2000	57.5%	0.03193955	2.7	$48,240	34.6	3.8	65.5
CO	2004	66.7%	0.030576014	5.4	$50,886	35.5	3.8	65.3
CO	2008	71.0%	0.029212478	4.8	$60,943	35.6	3.8	64.1
CO	2012	69.9%	0.108667348	8.1	$57,255	36.7	4.2	62.0
CO	2016	69.9%	0.176977029	3.9	$66,596	39.2	4.1	59.9
CT	2000	61.9%	0.025776169	2.3	$50,172	31.6	9.1	62.9
CT	2004	65.0%	0.021703581	4.9	$55,100	34.5	9.3	60.0
CT	2008	66.6%	0.017630993	5.7	$64,682	35.6	9.5	63.6
CT	2012	61.3%	0.064835496	8.4	$64,247	36.2	10.2	60.7
CT	2016	63.9%	0.08718003	5.6	$72,889	38.3	10.6	61.4
DE	2000	59.0%	-0.0252274	4.0	$50,365	24.0	19.2	63.8
DE	2004	64.2%	-0.03352501	3.9	$48,049	26.9	19.9	61.1
DE	2008	65.6%	-0.04182263	5.0	$50,702	27.5	20.6	59.9
DE	2012	62.3%	-0.00030644	7.2	$48,972	28.5	21.5	58.3
DE	2016	63.7%	0.01784236	5.0	$57,758	30.9	21.6	59.1
FL	2000	55.9%	0.001080066	3.6	$38,856	22.8	14.6	55.7
FL	2004	64.4%	-0.00357275	4.6	$40,535	26.0	15.0	55.4
FL	2008	66.1%	-0.00822556	6.1	$44,857	25.8	15.4	57.4

FL	2012	62.8%	-0.02683184	8.4	$46,071	26.2	16.1	55.5
FL	2016	64.5%	-0.00270936	5.4	$48,825	28.4	16.2	53.1
GA	2000	45.8%	-0.04081292	3.7	$41,901	23.1	28.7	63.3
GA	2004	56.2%	-0.03926453	4.7	$40,984	27.6	29.4	59.2
GA	2008	62.5%	-0.03771615	6.4	$46,227	27.5	30.0	60.4
GA	2012	59.0%	-0.03801054	9.1	$48,121	27.8	30.9	58.3
GA	2016	58.8%	-0.03412785	5.8	$50,768	29.9	31.3	55.4
HI	2000	44.2%	0.010332884	4.3	$51,546	26.3	1.8	62.6
HI	2004	48.2%	-0.00536549	3.4	$56,242	26.6	2.1	60.1
HI	2008	48.8%	-0.02106387	4.2	$61,521	29.1	2.4	59.9
HI	2012	44.2%	-0.01940248	6.0	$56,263	29.6	1.8	55.2
HI	2016	41.7%	-0.00789756	3.7	$64,514	31.4	2.1	57.6
ID	2000	57.2%	-0.08144955	4.9	$37,611	20.0	0.4	61.9
ID	2004	63.2%	-0.09200397	5.3	$44,358	23.8	0.5	61.3
ID	2008	63.6%	-0.1025584	5.4	$47,420	24.0	0.5	59.6
ID	2012	59.8%	-0.12267511	7.1	$47,922	24.7	0.5	56.5
ID	2016	59.4%	-0.04895868	4.3	$51,624	26.0	0.5	57.6
IL	2000	56.2%	-0.05180237	4.4	$46,064	27.1	15.1	63.1
IL	2004	61.5%	-0.10582883	6.1	$46,077	27.4	14.9	59.7
IL	2008	63.6%	-0.1598553	6.6	$53,254	29.9	14.6	61.0
IL	2012	58.9%	-0.00826898	8.7	$51,738	31.1	14.4	60.3
IL	2016	61.6%	0.060187417	5.9	$60,413	32.9	14.3	58.8
IN	2000	49.3%	0.092668105	3.2	$40,865	17.1	8.4	59.8
IN	2004	54.8%	0.062140228	5.3	$42,329	21.1	8.5	61.0

71

					$			
IN	2008	59.1%	0.03161235	6.0	46,520	22.9	8.6	60.5
IN	2012	55.2%	0.089714641	8.3	46,158	23.0	9.2	57.0
IN	2016	56.3%	0.150566589	4.8	51,983	24.9	9.1	58.5
IA	2000	63.2%	0.048462835	2.6	40,991	25.5	2.1	65.7
IA	2004	69.9%	0.022291022	4.6	43,391	24.3	2.3	65.4
IA	2008	69.4%	-0.00388079	4.0	50,142	24.3	2.5	67.5
IA	2012	70.3%	0.101707899	5.1	53,442	25.3	3.0	64.5
IA	2016	68.2%	0.105090698	3.6	60,855	26.8	3.4	65.7
KS	2000	55.6%	0.003856631	3.7	41,059	27.3	5.7	65.7
KS	2004	61.6%	-0.00308692	5.5	41,066	30.0	5.7	64.5
KS	2008	62.0%	-0.01003047	4.5	47,877	29.6	5.6	65.2
KS	2012	56.9%	-0.04066622	5.6	50,003	30.0	5.8	62.5
KS	2016	57.3%	0.053515953	4.3	54,865	31.7	5.9	61.6
KY	2000	52.2%	0.026402763	4.1	36,265	20.5	7.3	57.9
KY	2004	58.7%	0.008186148	5.2	35,610	21.0	7.4	55.4
KY	2008	57.9%	-0.01003047	6.3	41,148	19.7	7.4	54.6
KY	2012	55.7%	-0.10334456	8.0	41,086	21.0	7.9	55.8
KY	2016	58.7%	-0.10597756	5.4	42,387	23.3	8.0	51.7
LA	2000	56.4%	-0.00176607	5.5	30,718	22.5	32.5	54.2
LA	2004	61.1%	-0.01405611	6.0	36,429	22.4	32.2	54.9
LA	2008	61.2%	-0.02634615	5.0	39,563	20.3	31.9	55.9
LA	2012	60.2%	-0.0320419	7.1	39,085	21.4	32.2	52.9
LA	2016	59.8%	-0.02473835	6.2	45,922	23.2	32.2	55.4
ME	2000	67.2%	0.101269351	3.5	37,266	24.1	0.5	63.9

ME	2004	73.8%	0.09927568	4.7	$ 41,329	24.2	0.7	61.0
ME	2008	70.6%	0.097282009	5.4	$ 47,228	25.4	0.9	60.7
ME	2012	68.2%	0.159917747	7.7	$ 49,158	27.3	1.0	60.5
ME	2016	70.7%	0.161878543	4.4	$ 50,758	30.1	1.1	57.5
MD	2000	55.5%	-0.00246422	3.9	$ 54,535	32.3	27.9	64.3
MD	2004	62.9%	-0.02245848	4.2	$ 57,103	35.2	28.4	62.3
MD	2008	67.0%	-0.04245274	4.2	$ 63,711	35.2	28.9	64.0
MD	2012	66.6%	0.016927378	7.0	$ 71,836	36.3	29.2	63.7
MD	2016	66.2%	0.044556103	5.2	$ 73,594	38.8	29.5	62.2
MA	2000	59.9%	0.102632718	2.6	$ 46,753	32.7	5.4	61.4
MA	2004	64.2%	0.094883616	5.1	$ 52,019	36.7	5.9	61.9
MA	2008	66.8%	0.087134513	5.3	$ 60,320	38.1	6.3	61.4
MA	2012	65.9%	0.115579893	6.7	$ 63,656	39.0	7.1	61.7
MA	2016	66.8%	0.105822027	4.9	$ 67,861	41.5	7.3	61.0
MI	2000	59.9%	-0.01548337	3.6	$ 45,512	23.0	14.2	61.5
MI	2004	66.6%	-0.02741448	7.0	$ 42,256	24.4	14.1	59.7
MI	2008	69.2%	-0.0393456	8.3	$ 49,788	24.7	13.9	57.8
MI	2012	64.7%	-0.01817472	9.1	$ 50,015	25.5	14.0	54.5
MI	2016	64.6%	-0.01515719	5.4	$ 54,203	27.8	13.9	55.3
MN	2000	69.5%	0.105935949	3.3	$ 54,251	31.2	3.5	70.3
MN	2004	78.4%	0.083485692	4.8	$ 56,104	32.5	4.0	69.0
MN	2008	77.8%	0.061035435	5.5	$ 54,925	31.5	4.4	67.1
MN	2012	76.0%	0.066472048	5.8	$ 61,795	32.2	5.3	65.0
MN	2016	74.1%	0.122404232	3.8	$ 68,730	34.7	5.8	64.8

MS	2000	49.1%	-0.0503396	5.7	$ 34,299	18.7	36.3	57.0
MS	2004	55.7%	-0.08726973	6.2	$ 34,755	20.1	36.9	55.5
MS	2008	61.0%	-0.12419987	6.5	$ 36,446	19.4	37.5	53.9
MS	2012	59.3%	-0.09224543	8.9	$ 36,641	20.0	37.6	53.3
MS	2016	55.5%	-0.08661389	6.5	$ 40,037	20.8	37.7	51.3
MO	2000	58.2%	0.002437777	3.5	$ 45,097	26.2	11.2	64.3
MO	2004	65.3%	0.008313308	5.7	$ 42,137	28.1	11.2	62.7
MO	2008	67.60%	0.014188839	6.1	$ 46,038	25.0	11.1	60.7
MO	2012	62.20%	0.028690733	6.9	$ 49,764	25.8	11.5	59.3
MO	2016	62.10%	0.033640505	5.0	$ 59,196	27.8	11.7	60.6
MT	2000	61.60%	0.016804963	4.9	$ 32,777	23.8	0.3	64.3
MT	2004	64.40%	-0.01472938	4.9	$ 33,956	25.5	0.4	62.0
MT	2008	66.30%	-0.04626372	5.2	$ 42,900	27.1	0.5	63.0
MT	2012	62.50%	-0.02322974	6.1	$ 45,088	28.5	0.4	60.3
MT	2016	61.50%	0.059196072	4.1	$ 51,395	30.6	0.5	60.1
NE	2000	56.90%	-0.01360751	3.0	$ 41,750	24.6	4.0	69.0
NE	2004	62.90%	-0.02559677	3.8	$ 43,786	24.8	4.0	68.5
NE	2008	62.90%	-0.03758603	3.3	$ 50,728	27.1	4.0	68.1
NE	2012	60.30%	-0.02787047	4.0	$ 52,196	28.1	4.6	67.7
NE	2016	62.40%	-0.02535739	3.0	$ 60,474	30.2	4.8	64.1
NV	2000	45.20%	0.059996207	4.1	$ 45,758	19.3	6.8	63.0
NV	2004	55.30%	0.067458918	4.2	$ 47,204	24.5	7.1	59.3
NV	2008	57.00%	0.07492163	6.1	$ 54,744	21.9	7.4	62.2
NV	2012	56.40%	0.133931084	11.0	$ 47,333	22.2	8.3	58.4

74

NV	2016	57.10%	0.17157945	6.9	$ 52,008	23.6	8.5	57.2
NH	2000	63.90%	0.052877358	2.8	$ 50,926	30.1	0.7	66.7
NH	2004	70.90%	0.044619395	3.7	$ 56,815	35.4	0.9	64.7
NH	2008	71.70%	0.036361433	3.8	$ 66,176	33.3	1.0	65.6
NH	2012	70.20%	0.101679536	5.6	$ 67,819	33.4	1.3	64.7
NH	2016	71.50%	0.114097643	3.4	$ 75,675	35.7	1.6	63.7
NJ	2000	56.90%	-0.01126003	3.8	$ 50,405	30.1	13.6	58.4
NJ	2004	63.80%	-0.0129626	4.8	$ 55,275	34.6	13.6	58.4
NJ	2008	67.00%	-0.01466516	5.4	$ 65,306	34.4	13.6	60.2
NJ	2012	61.50%	0.021061988	9.5	$ 66,692	35.4	13.6	59.7
NJ	2016	63.60%	0.040551767	5.8	$ 68,357	37.6	13.4	56.9
NM	2000	48.50%	0.1529585	4.9	$ 35,093	23.6	1.9	57.2
NM	2004	59.00%	0.138686616	5.6	$ 39,562	25.1	2.1	57.5
NM	2008	60.90%	0.124414733	4.4	$ 42,102	24.7	2.3	58.1
NM	2012	54.60%	0.121129809	7.1	$ 43,424	25.6	2.1	54.9
NM	2016	54.70%	0.183401228	6.8	$ 45,119	26.5	2.3	52.5
NY	2000	55.10%	0.010662597	4.6	$ 40,744	28.7	15.9	56.1
NY	2004	58.00%	-0.01203553	5.8	$ 44,649	30.6	15.9	56.2
NY	2008	59.00%	-0.03473366	5.5	$ 50,461	31.9	15.9	56.9
NY	2012	53.10%	0.011628894	8.7	$ 47,680	32.8	15.6	55.7
NY	2016	55.70%	0.026758907	5.3	$ 58,005	35.0	15.6	55.1
NC	2000	50.70%	0.043342161	3.6	$ 38,317	23.2	21.6	61.6
NC	2004	57.80%	0.032753056	5.4	$ 40,238	23.4	21.4	58.8
NC	2008	65.50%	0.022163951	6.4	$ 42,930	26.1	21.2	58.2

75

NC	2012	64.80%	0.012237375	9.2	$41,553	26.8	21.6	56.1
NC	2016	64.80%	0.101442114	5.9	$50,797	29.4	21.6	56.0
ND	2000	60.30%	0.014350351	3.0	$35,996	22.6	0.6	67.0
ND	2004	64.80%	-0.0110232	3.4	$39,220	25.2	0.8	67.6
ND	2008	62.70%	-0.03639676	3.2	$49,631	26.9	1.0	70.1
ND	2012	59.80%	0.007208146	3.2	$55,766	27.1	1.5	67.6
ND	2016	59.10%	0.001599947	2.7	$57,415	29.1	2.1	64.9
OH	2000	56.70%	-0.01282734	4.1	$42,962	24.6	11.5	60.9
OH	2004	66.80%	-0.03521723	6.3	$43,055	24.6	11.6	60.4
OH	2008	66.90%	-0.05760711	6.5	$46,934	24.1	11.7	62.4
OH	2012	64.50%	-0.03853155	7.2	$44,375	24.7	12.2	57.8
OH	2016	62.80%	-0.03501442	4.9	$53,301	26.8	12.3	57.2
OK	2000	49.90%	-0.12082451	3.0	$32,432	22.5	7.6	57.3
OK	2004	58.30%	-0.11683065	4.9	$39,614	22.9	7.4	57.6
OK	2008	55.80%	-0.11283679	3.7	$46,111	22.2	7.2	56.0
OK	2012	49.20%	-0.04949813	5.1	$48,407	23.2	7.2	55.1
OK	2016	52.00%	0.024634593	4.3	$47,077	24.6	7.3	55.5
OR	2000	64.90%	0.060146193	4.9	$42,499	27.2	1.6	62.2
OR	2004	72.00%	0.046046897	7.6	$40,994	25.9	1.7	59.0
OR	2008	67.70%	0.0319476	6.4	$51,727	28.1	1.7	60.3
OR	2012	63.10%	0.037982545	8.9	$51,775	29.2	1.8	58.5
OR	2016	66.60%	0.059932315	5.7	$60,834	32.2	1.9	56.0
PA	2000	54.10%	0.016011725	4.2	$42,176	24.3	10.0	57.1
PA	2004	62.60%	-0.00212702	5.6	$44,106	25.3	10.2	58.1

PA	2008	63.60%	-0.02026577	5.3	$ 51,402	26.3	10.3	59.5
PA	2012	59.50%	-0.00037566	7.8	$ 51,904	27.0	11.0	57.9
PA	2016	62.80%	0.055870283	5.2	$ 60,389	29.7	11.0	57.7
RI	2000	54.20%	0.042326432	4.1	$ 42,197	26.4	4.5	60.6
RI	2004	58.50%	0.015006491	5.4	$ 47,935	27.2	5.0	61.7
RI	2008	61.80%	-0.01231345	7.9	$ 53,241	30.0	5.4	62.0
RI	2012	58.00%	0.051545135	10.5	$ 56,065	30.8	6.5	61.6
RI	2016	59.00%	0.075247796	5.9	$ 55,701	32.7	6.2	61.2
SC	2000	47.00%	0.011498517	3.9	$ 37,570	19.0	29.5	59.5
SC	2004	53.00%	-0.00455761	6.9	$ 38,691	24.9	28.8	59.5
SC	2008	58.00%	-0.02061374	6.7	$ 42,155	23.7	28.1	57.0
SC	2012	56.30%	-0.01522604	9.4	$ 44,401	24.6	27.7	54.9
SC	2016	56.80%	0.064845921	5.9	$ 46,360	26.8	27.5	55.0
SD	2000	57.70%	-0.08634808	2.3	$ 36,475	25.7	0.6	67.7
SD	2004	68.20%	-0.10036744	3.7	$ 41,107	25.5	0.8	69.4
SD	2008	64.70%	-0.11438679	3.0	$ 51,600	25.1	0.9	68.9
SD	2012	59.30%	-0.0702582	4.6	$ 49,415	26.0	1.6	64.2
SD	2016	58.50%	-0.07241581	3.5	$ 55,085	27.5	1.5	65.5
TN	2000	49.90%	0.028411128	3.9	$ 34,096	22.0	16.4	59.1
TN	2004	56.30%	0.003672261	5.1	$ 38,072	24.3	16.4	57.4
TN	2008	57.00%	-0.02106661	6.6	$ 39,702	22.9	16.3	56.6
TN	2012	51.90%	-0.03588021	7.8	$ 42,995	23.5	16.9	54.7
TN	2016	51.20%	-0.03121281	5.7	$ 47,330	25.7	16.8	52.9
TX	2000	49.20%	-0.08007041	4.2	$ 38,609	23.9	11.5	59.4

TX	2004	53.70%	-0.08940461	6.0	$ 41,397	24.5	11.5	58.2
TX	2008	54.10%	-0.09873881	4.8	$ 46,490	25.3	11.4	56.8
TX	2012	49.60%	-0.09600527	6.7	$ 51,926	26.3	11.9	57.7
TX	2016	51.20%	-0.09563494	4.4	$ 56,473	28.4	12.0	55.4
UT	2000	53.80%	-0.01866183	3.2	$ 47,550	26.4	0.8	62.7
UT	2004	58.90%	-0.03195508	5.3	$ 50,871	30.8	1.0	62.7
UT	2008	56.00%	-0.04524832	3.5	$ 62,537	29.1	1.1	60.7
UT	2012	55.50%	-0.05883007	5.8	$ 58,341	29.9	1.1	58.3
UT	2016	56.80%	0.013576553	3.6	$ 66,258	31.8	1.2	57.8
VT	2000	64.10%	0.053527105	2.9	$ 39,594	29.8	0.5	65.3
VT	2004	66.30%	0.052969787	3.7	$ 47,329	34.2	0.6	65.8
VT	2008	67.30%	0.05241247	4.9	$ 50,706	32.1	0.7	66.0
VT	2012	60.70%	0.088057729	5.1	$ 55,582	34.2	1.0	66.1
VT	2016	63.50%	0.109625888	3.6	$ 59,494	36.9	1.3	63.8
VA	2000	54.00%	-0.0642478	2.2	$ 47,163	31.9	19.6	61.3
VA	2004	60.60%	-0.09027625	3.9	$ 51,141	33.1	19.6	60.8
VA	2008	67.00%	-0.11630469	4.0	$ 61,985	33.7	19.6	64.2
VA	2012	66.10%	-0.07672934	6.0	$ 64,632	34.7	19.3	60.2
VA	2016	65.70%	0.002641844	4.5	$ 61,488	37.0	19.2	58.7
WA	2000	60.70%	0.052150123	5.2	$ 42,525	28.6	3.2	62.6
WA	2004	66.90%	0.046572619	6.2	$ 49,922	29.9	3.3	61.2
WA	2008	66.60%	0.040995116	5.3	$ 56,631	30.7	3.4	61.9
WA	2012	64.80%	0.132081034	8.3	$ 62,187	31.6	3.6	59.1
WA	2016	64.70%	0.160247364	5.6	$ 27,243	34.2	3.7	57.4

WV	2000	46.60%	0.088689411	5.5	$ 29,411	15.3	3.2	51.3
WV	2004	54.10%	0.02654798	5.3	$ 33,373	15.3	3.3	49.1
WV	2008	49.90%	-0.03559345	4.4	$ 37,994	17.1	3.4	50.3
WV	2012	46.30%	0.00047423	7.4	$ 43,553	17.9	3.3	48.9
WV	2016	49.90%	0.056802632	6.9	$ 42,824	19.6	3.9	48.0
WI	2000	67.60%	-0.03456522	3.5	$ 45,088	23.8	5.7	68.3
WI	2004	74.80%	-0.05502326	5.0	$ 45,732	25.6	5.8	66.6
WI	2008	72.40%	-0.0754813	4.7	$ 51,200	25.7	5.8	66.6
WI	2012	72.90%	-0.03607034	7.1	$ 53,079	26.4	6.3	64.7
WI	2016	69.30%	0.045431362	4.6	$ 55,425	28.4	6.3	63.7
WY	2000	59.20%	-0.0141735	3.9	$ 39,629	20.6	0.8	65.1
WY	2004	65.70%	-0.0390607	3.8	$ 45,397	22.5	1.0	65.3
WY	2008	62.80%	-0.0639479	2.9	$ 53,337	23.6	1.1	64.0
WY	2012	58.60%	-0.03824077	5.5	$ 57,512	24.3	1.0	62.3
WY	2016	59.40%	0.014550379	4.1	$ 60,925	26.2	0.8	61.2

Appendix B

Personal Freedom Weightings and Individual Components with Percentages

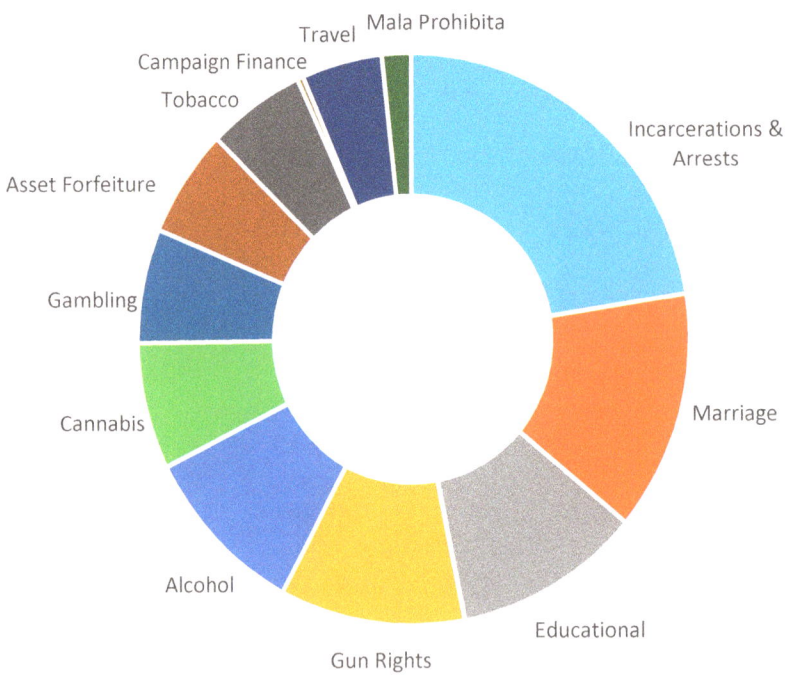

Incarceration and arrests: 6.6%

Crime-adjusted incarceration rate: 4.2%
Drug enforcement rate: 1.4%
Arrests for nondrug victimless crimes, % of population: 0.5%
Arrests for nondrug victimless crimes, % of all arrests: 0.5%

     The most heavily weighted category in the personal freedom dimension is the law enforcement statistics category, which consists of data on incarceration rates adjusted for violent and property crime rates, nondrug victimless crime arrests, and the drug enforcement rate. The personal freedom dimension also includes laws that create or reduce victimless crimes in other categories, such as marijuana, gun, and prostitution laws.

Marriage freedom: 4.0%

Same-sex partnerships laws: 2.2% Covenant marriage: 0.1%
Super-DOMA: 1.0% Blood test required: 0.01%
Sodomy laws: 0.4% T Total waiting period: 0.01%
Cousin marriage: 0.4%

Most of the weight of the marriage freedom category is tied to the availability of same-sex partnerships, both civil unions and marriage. The remainder is tied to waiting periods and blood test requirements, availability of cousin marriage and covenant marriage, and sodomy laws, which were struck down by the Supreme Court in 2003. Now that the Supreme Court has nationalized same-sex marriage, those distinctions among states may become irrelevant.

Education: 3.2%

Tax credit/deduction: 1.2% Homeschooling curriculum control: 0.04%
Publicly funded voucher law: 0.7% Homeschooling standardized testing: 0.03%
Private school teacher licensure: 0.6% Homeschooling record-keeping requirements: .03%
Private school approval requirement: 0.2% Homeschooling teacher qualifications: 0.01%
Compulsory schooling years: 0.2% Private school registration: <0.01%
Private school curriculum control: 0.2% Homeschool statute: <0.01%
Public school choice: 0.1%

Gun control: 3.2%

Local gun ban: 1.0% Nonpowder guns: 0.03%
Concealed-carry index: 0.4% Restrictions on multiple purchases: 0.03%
Initial permit cost: 0.4% Background checks for private sales: 0.02%
Firearms licensing index: 0.3% Registration of firearms: 0.02%
Waiting period for purchases: 0.3% Design safety standards: 0.01%
Initial permit term: 0.2% Machine guns: 0.01%
Stricter minimum age: 0.2% Ammo microstamping: 0.01%
Assault weapons ban: 0.1% Large-capacity magazine bans: 0.01%
Open carry index: 0.05% Sound suppressor: <0.01%
No duty to retreat: 0.05% Short-barreled shotguns: <0.01%
Any other weapon: 0.04% Short-barreled rifles: <0.01%
Dealer licensing: 0.03% 50 caliber ban: <0.01%
Built-in locking devices: 0.03%

Alcohol: 2.9%

Alcohol distribution index: 1.1%
Blue law index: 0.4%
Sales and grocery stores: 0.4%
Spirits taxes: 0.3%
Wine taxes: 0.2%

Beer taxes: 0.2%
Direct wine shipment ban: 0.2%
Keg regulations/ban: 0.1%
Happy hour ban: 0.03%
Mandatory server training: <0.01%

Marijuana Freedom: 2.1%

Medical marijuana index: 0.9%
Possession decriminalization: 0.6%
Marijuana misdemeanor index: 0.1%

Mandatory minimums: 0.1%
Some sales legal: 0.1%
Salvia ban: 0.1%

Gambling: 1.9%

Gaming revenues: 1.8%
Gambling felony: 0.02%

Social gambling: 0.02%
Internet gaming prohibition: <0.01%

Asset forfeiture: 1.8%
Asset forfeiture law: 0.9%
Equitable sharing: 0.9%

Civil asset forfeiture is the government's ability to take a person's property by accusing him or her of a crime. Often the seized cash or proceeds of auctioning the property accrue to the seizing agency, providing incentives for "policing for profit." Typically, the person whose property is seized must file suit and prove innocence to get the property back. Both federal and state/local law enforcement engage in asset forfeiture.

Tobacco 1.7%

Cigarette tax: 1.3%
Smoking ban, bars: 0.3%
Internet purchase regulations: 0.06%

Smoking ban, private workplaces: 0.03%
Smoking ban, restaurants: 0.03%
Vending machine regulations: 0.03%

Travel freedom: 1.4%

Automated license plate readers: 0.4%
Motorcycle helmet law: 0.1%
Seat belt laws: 0.2%

Sobriety checkpoints: 0.2%
Cell phone ban: 0.01%
Open-container law: 0.01%

Fingerprint for driver's license: 0.1%
Uninsured/underinsured coverage requirement: 0.1%
Driver's licenses without Social Security number: 0.3%

Mala prohibit a and civil liberties: 0.5%

Prostitution legal: 0.2%
Trans-fat bans: 0.1%
Raw milk legal: 0.1%
Mixed martial arts legal: 0.1%
Religious Freedom Restoration Act: 0.01%

Fireworks laws: 0.05%
Physician-assisted suicide legal: 0.03%
Equal rights amendment: 0.02%
DNA database index: 0.01%

The term mala prohibit a refers to acts defined as criminal in statute, even though they are not harms in common law (mala in se). This category is a grab bag of mostly unrelated policies, including raw milk laws, fireworks laws, prostitution laws, physician-assisted suicide laws, religious freedom restoration acts, rules on taking DNA samples from criminal suspects without a probable-cause hearing, trans-fat bans, and, new to the 2016 edition, state equal rights amendments, and mixed martial arts legalization.

Campaign finance: 0.1%

Individual contributions to candidates: 0.03%
Individual contributions to parties: 0.02%
Grassroots PAC contributions to candidates: 0.02%
Grassroots PAC contributions to parties: 0.01%
Public financing: <0.01%

By regulating contributions to parties and candidates, governments effectively limit citizens' ability to spread their ideas, thereby limiting their personal freedom.

Lightning Source UK Ltd.
Milton Keynes UK
UKHW051539091019

351284UK00002B/21/P